PSHE Education 3

Lesley de Meza

Stephen De Silva

DL **DYNAMIC** LEARNING

HODDER
EDUCATION
AN HACHETTE UK COMPANY

Orders: please contact Bookpoint Ltd, 130 Milton Park, Abingdon, Oxon OX14 4SB. Telephone: +44 (0)1235 827720. Fax: +44 (0)1235 400454. Lines are open 9.00–5.00, Monday to Saturday, with a 24-hour message answering service. Visit our website at www.hoddereducation.co.uk.

© Lesley de Meza and Stephen De Silva, 2010
First published in 2010 by
Hodder Education,
An Hachette UK company
338 Euston Road
London NW1 3BH

Impression number   10 9 8 7 6 5 4 3 2 1
Year   2014 2013 2012 2011 2010

Cover photo © Pixland/Corbis
Layouts by Julie Martin
Artwork by Richard Duszczak, Karen Donnelly, Dylan Gibson, Stephanie Strickland and Barking Dog Art
Printed and bound in Italy

A catalogue record for this title is available from the British Library

ISBN: 978 0 340 94724 1

Acknowledgements

The Publishers would like to thank the following for permission to reproduce copyright material:

Photo credits
p.4 © Andres Rodriguez – Fotolia.com; **p.7** 1 © Steve Niedorf Photography/Stone/Getty Images, 2 © Ricky John Molloy/Taxi/Getty Images, 3 © Stockbyte/Getty Images; **p.8** © Image Source/Alamy; **p.10** 1 © Imagestate Media, 2 © Janine Wiedel Photolibrary/Alamy, 3 © EPS/Rex Features, 4 © Photodisc/Getty Images, 5 © Tomaz Levstek/iStockphoto.com; **p.14** l–r 1 © Ian Shaw/Alamy, 2 © Wave Royalty Free/Alamy, 3 © Visions of America, LLC/Alamy; **p.15** t © Visions of America, LLC/Alamy, m © Robert Fried/Alamy, b © Dale O'Dell/Alamy; **pp.16–17** © Etienne Ansotte/Rex Features; **p.18** © Bubbles Photolibrary/Alamy; **p.20** Courtesy of Citizen's Advice Bureau; **p.23** Courtesy of Help the Hospices/www.helpthehospices.org.uk; **p.26** l–r 1 © John Powell/Rex Features, 2 © Angela Hampton Picture Library/Alamy, 3 © Leila Cutler/Alamy; **p.30** l–r 1 © Ace Stock Limited/Alamy, 2 © 1995 Jack Star/PhotoDisc/Getty Images, 3 © Imagestate Media, 4 © Creatas/Comstock/Photolibrary.com; **p.32** l–r t1 © Stuart Clarke/Rex Features, t2 © 1995 PhotoLink/Photodisc/Getty Images, t3 © AGF s.r.l./Rex Features, t4 © vario images GmbH & Co.KG/Alamy, b1 © B.A.E. Inc./Alamy, b2 © Alan Pembleton/Alamy, b3 © Imagestate Media, b4 © Paul Melling/Alamy; **p.34** l Courtesy of Talpa Products, r © Nick Cunard/Rex Features; **p.36** © Jonathan Banks/Rex Features; **p.37** t Courtesy of Unilever, b Ready Brek advert courtesy of Weetabix. Ready Brek is the registered trademark of Weetabix Limited; **p.38** t © The Print Collector/Alamy, b © Brand X/Photolibrary Group Ltd; **p.39** t–b 1 © VStock/Alamy, 2 © UK Stock Images Ltd/Alamy, 3 © Catherine Yeulet/iStockphoto.com; **p.41** 1 & 2 © Brand X/Photolibrary Group Ltd, 3 © UpperCut Images/Alamy; **p.43** l © Redfx/Alamy, r © Steve Taylor ARPS/Alamy; **p.44** © John Fryer/Alamy; **p.45** © Jeff Morgan 11/Alamy; **p.49** t © David Bebber/WPA Pool/Getty Images, m © Brand X/Photolibrary Group Ltd, b © Ian Shaw/Alamy; **p.51** © Radius Images/Alamy; **p.53** © Mark Sykes/Alamy; **p.55** A © Stockbyte/Getty Images, B © Hank Morgan/Science Photo Library, C © Pulse Picture Library/Press Association Images, D © Scott Camazine/Science Photo Library, E © Saturn Stills/Science Photo Library, F © Image Source/Alamy; **p.56** tr © Bettina Strenske/Alamy, bl © Janine Wiedel Photolibrary/Alamy; **p.58** A © Allstar Picture Library/Alamy, B © North Wind Picture Archives/Alamy, C © Life Magazine/Time & Life Pictures/Getty Images,

D © Rex Features, E © Ray Tang/Rex Features, F © John Downing/Rex Features; **p.59** © Rex Features; **p.61** l–r t1 © Darrin Jenkins/Alamy, t2 © Imagestate Media, t3 © GustoImages/Science Photo Library, t4 © Rex Features, t5 © Sakki/Rex Features, b1 © Action Press/Rex Features, b2 © Tek Image/Science Photo Library, b3 © Mykel Nicolaou/Rex Features, b4 © Cristina Pedrazzini/Science Photo Library; **p.67** tl © Juice Images/Alamy, tr © Paul Burns/Blend Images/Getty Images, bl © Voisin/Phanie/Rex Features, br © Radius Images/Alamy; **p.69** Clockwise from top 1 © K-Photos/Alamy, 2 © Larry Lilac/Alamy, 3 © Letterbox Digital/Alamy, 4 © Ace Stock Limited/Alamy, 5 © Jim West/Alamy, 6 © RTimages/Alamy, 7 © K-Photos/Alamy.

t = top, b = bottom, l = left, r = right

Text acknowledgements
p.7 International Olympic Committee for list of Canadian Olympic Values from www.olympicschool.ca; **p.22** David Twigg on behalf of Management Committee of Aghalee Village Hall for case study; **p.31** web extracts from www.wiseguys.org.uk; **p.33** report from www.goodwithmoney.co.uk/ethical-consumerism-report-08; **p.43** Penguin Books Ltd for Allan Ahlberg, 'Picking Teams' from Please Mrs Butler (Kestrel Books, 1983); **p.44** Changing Faces for web extract on Jessica Lee from www.iface.org.uk; Gordon Poole Agency for case study of Tanni Grey Thompson adapted from www.youtube.com; **p.45** University Press of Mississippi for case study of Maya Angelou from Conversations with Maya Angelou, edited by Jeffrey M. Elliot (Virago, 1989); **p.46** Patrick Tolan for extracts from 'It's All Relative' from www.poemhunter.com/poem/it-s-all-relative-2; **p.49** extract from speech by Prince William to Child Bereavement Charity, March 2009.

Every effort has been made to trace all copyright holders, but if any have been inadvertently overlooked the Publishers will be pleased to make the necessary arrangements at the first opportunity.

Although every effort has been made to ensure that website addresses are correct at time of going to press, Hodder Education cannot be held responsible for the content of any website mentioned in this book. It is sometimes possible to find a relocated web page by typing in the address of the home page for a website in the URL window of your browser.

Contents

How will we work together?

In this lesson you will:
★ **learn about the five Every Child Matters outcomes**
★ **negotiate ways of working together**
★ **consider your personal qualities, skills and achievements.**

Starter activity

You are now in the final year of Key Stage 3 and can probably think back over the many changes you have experienced since you started this Key Stage.

You might be considering what the future holds for you. When young people across the country were asked about their hopes for the future they said that they would like to:

● be healthy
● stay safe
● enjoy and achieve
● make a positive contribution
● achieve economic wellbeing.

What sorts of things do you think those young people meant by each of these hopes?

All the chapters in this book are based around these five hopes or goals. They are the five national outcomes known as Every Child Matters. Working towards these outcomes will happen both individually and as part of group work during activities you take part in within and outside school. The Every Child Matters out comes were decided following consultation with young people. The five outcomes sum up what they hoped the future would hold for them.

Get Active 1

Working together as a group happens best when we use a Group Agreement. You will probably be familiar with this from last year's PSHE education course.

Source 1 opposite is an example of a Group Agreement. Is there anything you would want to change about it? Think about things to add, things to leave out or things to amend.

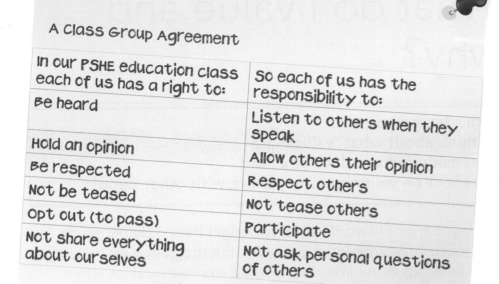

A Class Group Agreement

In our PSHE education class each of us has a right to:	So each of us has the responsibility to:
Be heard	Listen to others when they speak
Hold an opinion	Allow others their opinion
Be respected	Respect others
Not be teased	Not tease others
Opt out (to pass)	Participate
Not share everything about ourselves	Not ask personal questions of others

Source 1

Whilst you are a member of the class who shares this Group Agreement, you are also an individual with your own thoughts, feelings and unique personality.

It isn't always easy to find the words to explain what makes you special but each person is!

Get Active 2

There are lots of ways of expressing yourself as an individual. In this activity you are going to produce an illustration to express yourself. This could take the form of:

- a coat of arms
- part of a patchwork quilt
- a badge that could be worn on clothing or on a bag/rucksack.

Or you could think of another way of displaying your ideas. Whichever way you choose, try to include at least seven of the following:

- your name (and its meaning if you know it)
- words that describe you
- your favourite place
- your favourite TV programme/book/radio programme
- a career you would like to pursue
- hobbies and activities you enjoy
- one of your achievements
- one thing you like about yourself
- your motto.

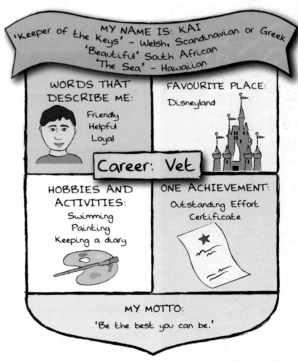

Source 2

Source 2 shows an example of a coat of arms based on some that people your age have produced. It may give you ideas but make sure that your work is as individual as you are.

Get Active 3

Look back at the five national outcomes for Every Child Matters in the Starter Activity opposite. Which one of them would you say you are on the way to achieving and how are you getting there?

What do I value and why?

In this lesson you will:
★ **think about what 'values' are**
★ **consider what values *you* hold**
★ **reflect on values you may share with other people.**

When you hear the word 'value' you might think it simply means how much money something is worth. But the truth is we value all kinds of things in our lives, in lots of different ways. Think about whether or not any of these things are worth anything to you:

• having a good friend
• being able to talk to a family member you trust
• the pleasure you get from having a pet
• finding time to watch TV or listen to music
• having the freedom to express your opinion.

Starter activity

Imagine someone who says:

I value planet Earth and have concerns about global warming – so I do my best to support organisations that stop the destruction of the rainforests. For example, I only use recycled paper.

This person has a value that affects the way they behave. What value or values do you hold that makes you act in a certain way?

Most people have a range of values that influence the way they think, feel and behave. Some values will be more important to them than others.

Get Active 1

Look at Source 1 opposite. It shows Zoe at the centre and around her are two circles showing six things she really values – three of them are particularly important and those are shown closest to her.

Construct your own values circle with you at the centre and two more rings of values surrounding you.

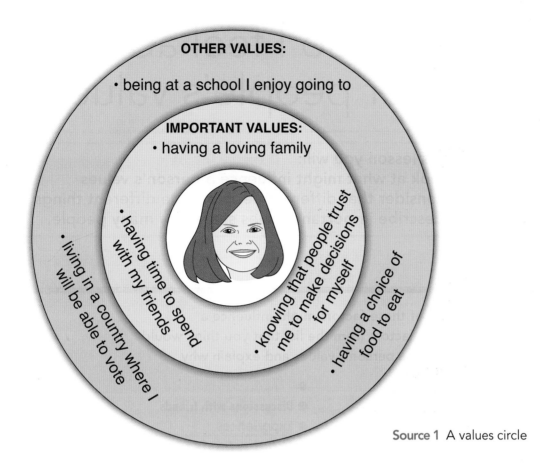

OTHER VALUES:

• being at a school I enjoy going to

IMPORTANT VALUES:
• having a loving family

• having time to spend with my friends

• living in a country where I will be able to vote

• knowing that people trust me to make decisions for myself

• having a choice of food to eat

Source 1 A values circle

Get Active 2

By now you will have a clearer idea of some of the things you value. This activity asks you to think about the bigger picture.

1 Look at the values listed below:
   a) Being free to express our opinions
   b) Enjoying ourselves
   c) Having human rights
   d) Feeling safe
   e) Having rules and laws
   f) Being free to have our own beliefs
   g) Having good health services
   h) Having respect
   i) Being trusted

   These are the values we often share in our communities and the society in which we live. Which of the values is most important to you?

2 Look at Source 2 on the right. It shows a Diamond Nine arrangement for placing things in a priority order.

   Sort the nine values from part 1, placing the one of most value to you in position 1 and the one of least value in position 9.

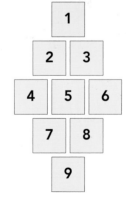

Source 2 A Diamond Nine

Get Active 3

Look at the nine values in Get Active 2 above. If you could only choose one to have in your life, what would your most prized value be – and why?

3 What do I feel about other people's values?

In this lesson you will:
★ look at what might influence a person's values
★ consider that different people value different things
★ describe important values shared by many people.

Starter activity

Look at the list below. Which of these factors might influence a person's values? Choose three factors from the list that you think would have the strongest influence on a person's values and explain why.

- Views of parents/carers
- The law
- Religious teachings
- NEWSPAPERS/TELEVISION/ THE INTERNET

- National traditions
- Discussions with friends
- Experiences
- *What schools teach*

All of the above factors are influences which can shape people's values. We don't all experience exactly the same influences in our lives – so we may find that we share some values with others but sometimes also have very individual values.

Having different values from others is something we discover as we get older and meet an increasingly wider variety of people outside our own circle of family and close friends.

Get Active 1

By now you will understand that we don't all value the same things. Take a couple of minutes to think about how you would respond to the three questions below, then share your thoughts with another member of the class. Were there values you had in common? Were there values you felt differently about?

1 What things do you value for yourself? (For example, being honest or kind.)
2 What things do you value for others? (This means it may not apply in your life but you can see it as having value for others. For example, being a good sportsman/woman; enjoying cooking.)
3 What things do you not value for yourself and others? (For example, being violent or unkind.)

Get Active 2

You have had an opportunity to compare your values with another person. This activity gives you a chance to see how you may agree or differ in your values with the rest of the class.

Look at the three value statements in Source 1.

- How do you feel about the values expressed in each statement?
- What reasons can you give for feeling that way?
- Hold a class vote to find out what the whole class thinks.

Values should influence the way we meet, work and live with others in a positive way. A good example of this can be seen every four years when people from countries across the world come together to compete in the Olympic Games. The Olympic and Paralympic Movements extend well beyond the Games themselves. Athletes performing at the highest level – or in training to get there – are encouraged to live by a set of shared principles, or ways of living. Whatever country they come from, each person is asked to embrace a set of values which help nations and competitors get the most out of the Games.

Get Active 3

Look at Source 2 below and explain each one. It lists the values that the Canadian Olympic Committee believes in and explains each one. Below are the values of the London 2012 Olympics. For each value, write a sentence that explains it.

The Olympic and Paralympic Values – London 2012:

- Friendship
- Respect
- Determination
- Inspiration
- Equality
- Courage
- Excellence

Get Active 4

There are seven values listed in Get Active 3. What eighth value would you choose for the Olympic Movement and why? You can only use one word.

1 Relationships: parents should be able to approve whoever you go out with

2 Community: senior citizens should always move to the front of the queue

3 Food: eating vegetables and not eating meat or animal products is better for everyone

Source 2
The Canadian Olympic Values – see
www.olympicschool.ca

Lesson 3 What do I feel about other people's values?

Excellence
We believe in the right of all people to go after their personal levels of excellence.

Fairness
We believe in fairness on and off the field of play, through equality and trust.

Respect
We believe in open communication and respect for the views, roles and contributions of all.

Fun
We believe in sport being fun.

Personal growth
We believe that the physical, social, mental and spiritual wellbeing of all should be improved through appropriate behaviour and practices. We also believe that the visual and performing arts complement sport and the wellbeing of the athletes.

Leadership
We believe those who participate in sport have a responsibility to teach and apply the values of the Olympic Movement. They should also involve others in the Olympic experience and inspire and empower them to reach their potential.

Peace
We believe in sport as a way to promote understanding and harmony within nations.

How do I improve my career prospects?

In this lesson you will:
★ **think about the types of jobs and careers that are available to you**
★ **consider what motivates people to work**
★ **identify what factors will motivate you.**

Most people work at some time in their lives. There are various reasons for working and for the majority of people it's because they need to earn money so that they can survive in society. Some people get extra job satisfaction because they enjoy the work that they do. Employers are keen to have people working for them who are motivated.

Starter activity

Why do you think it is important to be motivated by what you do? Try to think of at least five reasons.

Source 1 What motivates me to work?

Relationships – enjoying being with the people you work with; having self-respect.

Self-fulfilment – personal satisfaction, for example feeling that you are doing something interesting and worthwhile.

Material comforts – the things you can buy with your salary, for example holidays, clothing, a car, etc.

Security – a secure job where you are unlikely to be made redundant.

Status – gaining personal recognition; being in charge.

Get Active 1

Look at Source 1. It's not always possible to get each of these five things from one job. If you had to put the factors in order, which one would be most important to you – and why?

Form your own personal priority order in the shape of the Diamond Five on the right. The top factor should be the most important to you; the bottom position should show the least important factor to you.

Get Active 2

Now that you have thought about what motivates you to work, what would that mean for your chosen career? What would it look like?

Look at Source 2 below. Copy and complete the following table by placing each statement from Source 2 under the heading you think it fits best. Explain why you think it fits there.

Material comforts	Status	Relationships	Security	Self-fulfilment

Source 2 What do I want from my job?

a) To look after people	**b)** To work as part of a team	**c)** To be my own boss	**d)** To manage other people	**e)** Long summer holidays	**f)** Annual bonus payments
g) To decide how and when to do work	**h)** To stay in the same job for working life	**i)** To have good work colleagues	**j)** Not to have to take my work home with me	**k)** To be offered new opportunities	**l)** To receive recognition for my work
m) To get overtime payments	**n)** To be respected by fellow workers	**o)** To have good promotion prospects	**p)** To have good long-term prospects	**q)** To travel and stay in the best hotels	**r)** To do interesting work
s) To receive on-the-job training	**t)** To have a high level of responsibility	**u)** To get a new company car each year	**v)** To deal directly with customers	**w)** To receive good wages	**x)** To be able to see the results of my work

Get Active 3

1 Look at the table headings from Get Active 2. Choose the heading that represents the most important motivation you identified in your Diamond Five in Get Active 1.

2 Now look at the statements that you placed underneath the heading – think of any types of jobs/careers that will give you the motivation and job satisfaction you are looking for.

Get Active 4

Look at Source 3 – the SMART Targets. Now write down a specific next step for yourself that fits one of the SMART Target criteria and will help you on your way to your future career.

Source 3 SMART Targets

S **Specific** (e.g. I will base my options choices on subjects I enjoy and can achieve in)
M **Measurable** (e.g. I will be on time each day this term)
A **Attainable** (e.g. I will finish projects by their deadline)
R **Realistic** (e.g. I will research which qualifications I need for my career path)
T **Time specific** (e.g. I will achieve these targets by the date I have to choose my options)

5 What's out there?

> **In this lesson you will:**
> ★ **think about the skills, qualities and abilities needed for employment**
> ★ **learn about different employment categories/families**
> ★ **assess some of your own skills and abilities.**

Source 1

Starter activity

Look at the photographs in Source 1. What work settings do you think these people and jobs belong in? Look at the list in Source 2 for some ideas of different types of work settings.

'What do you want to be when you grow up, dear?' is a question that many young people get asked time and time again … especially by relatives we only see once a year! There's no need to decide right now whether you want to be a brain surgeon or a nightclub bouncer. You're likely to succeed in doing things that you enjoy and are good at.

So you don't have to choose a career just yet but it may be helpful to think about the different options open in various work settings.

There are many different types of work settings – these are sometimes called employment 'sectors', 'categories' or 'families', as listed in Source 2. Within each sector there are lots of different types of jobs. Working in different sectors requires different sets of skills.

Source 2 Employment categories/families

Administration, business and office work	Building and construction	Catering and hospitality
Computers and IT	Design, arts and crafts	Education and training
Engineering	Environment, animals and plants	Financial services
Healthcare	Languages, information and culture	Legal and political services
Leisure, sport and tourism	Manufacturing and production	Marketing and advertising
Media, print and publishing	Performing arts	Personal and other services (including hair and beauty)
Retail sales and customer services	Science, mathematics and statistics	Security and armed forces
Social work and counselling services	Transport and logistics	

You can find more information about the jobs in the Careers Reference Library Connexions Index at: www.cegnet.co.uk/files/CEGNET0001/crciresources/a2_index.xls

Get Active 1

Working in pairs, look at the list of employment categories/families (taken from the Careers Reference Library Connexions Index) in Source 2 opposite. What skills, abilities and qualities do you think someone working in one of the categories/families would need?

For example, someone working in the health sector might be described like as having the following attributes:

- skills – being accurate and giving attention to detail; communication skills
- abilities – good at thinking in a scientific way; knowledge of human biology
- qualities – care about health of others and desire to help them.

You will by now have realised that there are many opportunities open to you that need a variety of skills, abilities and qualities. You may already have recognised some of these skills and qualities within yourself – and there may be others you want to develop.

Get Active 2

1 Below are three employment categories/ families. In groups, look at the one your teacher allocates to you.

- Environment, animals and plants
- Media, print and publishing
- Leisure, sport and tourism

Discuss the skills, qualities and abilities you think a Year 9 pupil may already have that will enable them to choose a job in that sector.

2 Now discuss what the Year 9 pupil could plan to do in Years 10 and 11 to help them further their path in that direction. For example, what sort of job would it be useful to take on for work experience? What qualifications would it be helpful to gain? Think about things like: GCSE, GNVQ, BTEC, Diploma, WorkSkills, A level or IB.

Now that you've considered this process for people who might be thinking about the three sectors above, the next activity encourages you to think about yourself.

Get Active 3

What are you good at and what do you enjoy? Look at the chart in Source 3 below. Find four 'Can you' questions to which you can answer 'yes'. For each one, give examples of how you could demonstrate this. Answering the questions in the chart should help you to assess your own skills and abilities.

Get Active 4

Think back over what you have done in this lesson and complete this sentence: 'Based on today's lesson I could …'

Source 3 Assessing your own skills and abilities

What 'people skills' do you have? Can you:	What can you do creatively? Can you:	What practical things are you good at? Can you:	What are your data skills? Can you:
'sell' ideas or things to people?	design things?	fix things?	analyse information?
perform in front of people?	draw and paint?	build things?	think of ways to solve problems?
listen to people?	write?	use tools?	read and research things?
organise people?	compose?	assemble and put together things?	manage money?
be sensitive to people's feelings?	come up with new and exciting ideas?		use maths skills in everyday situations?
teach people?		do physical things?	organise things?
help people develop ideas?			follow instructions?

6 What are my options?

> **In this lesson you will:**
> ★ think about the subjects you are currently studying and those you will study next year
> ★ identify some ways of planning how to choose options for the future
> ★ consider how you might make a good start on new courses.

Starter activity

If now was the time when you could choose subjects you find interesting, challenging, and enjoyable, what subjects would you choose and why?

IB
GCSE
A Level
Diploma
GNVQ
?
ASDAN

When it comes to choosing option subjects, not all schools follow exactly the same methods. However, you will have to make a choice at some point. Most schools get you ready for this with a range of activities. These are the sorts of things that could be available to you:

- **Options evenings** – you will have an opportunity to talk to subject teachers about your ideas and what they think.

- **Information about subjects and courses** – this could be available in a booklet or on your school's website.

- **One to one discussions** – you can talk with your teachers, form tutor and perhaps mentors.

- **Careers advice** – careers advice should be available in school so that you can discuss any plans you might have for the future.

- **Taster sessions and/or activity days** – you might be offered the chance to try out subjects and courses or you could be given the chance to take part in games, challenges or lessons linked to Year 9 choices.

Get Active 1

Your school will offer you some or all of the above ways of planning your choices for next year. Working in pairs, discuss the following questions:

1 What can you do to get the most out of these events?

2 Who would be good to talk to about your decision?

  - A family member
  - Someone doing a job you might be interested in
  - Who else?

3 What questions could you ask?

Your school will probably offer a choice of qualifications for different subjects. What you choose will probably depend on your hopes for your future.

The most important thing is that you don't rush into making a choice without proper thinking and planning.

Get Active 2

1 When thinking ahead it's a good idea to be clear about your strengths and how you learn best. Take a look at the lists below and identify which apply to you.

I am ...	I learn best by ...
• creative	• seeing and reading
• enterprising	• listening and talking
• investigative	• touching and doing
• organised	• doing projects
• practical	• doing tasks
• sociable	

2 Having considered the way you learn, go on to look at the options open to you by answering the following questions:

a) What subjects will I have to do (compulsory or core)?

b) What subjects am I interested in and why?

c) What subjects don't interest me and what are the reasons for this?

d) Are there new subjects that sound interesting to me?

3 Now that you have thought about your individual needs, discuss the following in groups:

a) Are there pros and cons to basing our choices on what friends are choosing rather than considering our own strengths and what we need for our future?

b) Should we choose subjects based on having favourite teachers because we'd like to do their subject, even if we are not very good at it?

c) Would it be wise to choose a subject just because it sounds glamorous or exciting?

Lots of us have fantasies and dreams about what we would like to do in the future. The reality for all of us will be about finding a balance between our abilities, the effort we put in and what is feasible. Not everyone will be able to be a famous pop star or premier league footballer … and not everyone will want to.

Whichever career path you decide to follow, you will need to gain practical or vocational skills or academic qualifications so that you are able to demonstrate why you are the best person for the job you want.

Starting on courses that lead to qualifications can feel intimidating or not much fun compared to the work you are doing now – but there are some sensible and practical things a person can do to help them cope with these new demands.

Get Active 3

Read Source 1. What other good advice would you give someone to help them study better?

Source 1 Success with studying

> Many of the subjects you'll be studying in the years ahead will include work you will be expected to complete on your own and often in your own time. You're much more likely to succeed if you:
>
> - find somewhere to study where you won't be disturbed
> - choose topics that interest you – this will keep you enthusiastic
> - get organised – plan carefully and give yourself plenty of time to complete your work
> - research your subject matter carefully – undertake as much research as possible before you start writing up. But don't plagiarise (copy other people's work and pretend it's your own)
> - when you write up your work, ensure it is clear and neat. Always check your spelling, grammar and punctuation before handing it in.

Get Active 4

If you could ask only one question about transition to a sixth-form student (from Years 12 or 13), what would it be? Why is that the most important question?

7

What makes a successful community?

In this lesson you will:
★ think about the communities you belong to
★ identify some guidelines for successful community life
★ consider the qualities that improve community life.

Source 1 Looking after the community

Think back to Lesson 1 in this book. As a class you negotiated a Group Agreement based on rights and responsibilities. This was a type of 'community contract' where you gained rights and at the same time contributed by taking on responsibilities.

Get Active 1

Source 1 shows individuals looking after their community. Each of us individually gains from being part of a community – and there are things we already do (or should be doing) so that other members of the community benefit as well. Take one of your example communities from the Starter Activity and list three things you gain from being part of that community and three things you contribute to it.

Imagine a futuristic experiment which involves setting up a colony of earth (Novo-Earth) on a new planet. A representative selection of people from across the world has been chosen to take part in this new community. They include people with the variety of skills needed to set up a society, for example teachers, doctors, engineers, etc. You are amongst the teenagers included. Everyone has a vital role to play and has been chosen because they are able to contribute to this new community.

The people of Novo-Earth will need to set up rules and guidelines to live by. Although these people come from many different countries on Earth they all share Earth's Universal Declaration of Human Rights. As part of the consultation process you have been invited to put forward three rules or guidelines that uphold some of the Human Rights in the Declaration.

Source 2 Life in the new community of Novo-Earth

Get Active 2

1 In groups, work on one of the categories below, which your teacher will allocate to you.

- Education
- Health and wellbeing
- Equality
- Employment
- Freedom of thought/belief

2 Read the articles on pages 16 and 17: 'The Universal Declaration of Human Rights – some selected articles'.

3 For your allocated category, use your own words to explain three rules or guidelines for Novo-Earth that you think uphold some of the relevant points in the Universal Declaration of Human Rights.

4 Give feedback on your three points to the rest of the class.

5 Individually decide on which of the points in each category is the most important and take a class vote to decide the top guideline in each category. This should give you five key rules/guidelines for the new community.

Not all of the rules we live by are written down – culturally many groups have evolved informal ways of behaving that encourage harmony. For example, being courteous; respecting people who are different; helping neighbours; and so on.

Get Active 3

Look at Source 1 opposite. Leaving laws and guidelines aside, what ways of behaving would you like to see that would promote harmony and wellbeing?

Get Active 4

Sometimes people talk about living by their 'golden rule', for example 'Treat other people as you would like to be treated'. What would be your one golden rule and why?

TREAT OTHER PEOPLE AS YOU WOULD LIKE TO BE TREATED

The Universal Declaration of Human Rights – some selected articles

Article 1

All human beings are born free and equal in dignity and rights. They are endowed with reason and conscience and should act towards one another in a spirit of brotherhood.

Article 2

Everyone is entitled to all the rights and freedoms set forth in this Declaration, without distinction of any kind, such as race, colour, sex, language, religion, political or other opinion, national or social origin, property, birth or other status.

Article 3

Everyone has the right to life, liberty and security of person.

Article 4

No one shall be held in slavery or servitude; slavery and the slave trade shall be prohibited in all their forms.

Article 5

No one shall be subjected to torture or to cruel, inhuman or degrading treatment or punishment.

Article 6

Everyone has the right to recognition everywhere as a person before the law.

Article 7

All are equal before the law and are entitled without any discrimination to equal protection of the law.

Article 8

Everyone has the right to an effective remedy by the competent national tribunals for acts violating the fundamental rights granted him by the constitution or by law.

Article 9

No one shall be subjected to arbitrary arrest, detention or exile.

Article 10

Everyone is entitled in full equality to a fair and public hearing by an independent and impartial tribunal, in the determination of his rights and obligations and of any criminal charge against him.

Article 11

Everyone charged with a penal offence has the right to be presumed innocent until proved guilty according to law in a public trial at which he has had all the guarantees necessary for his defence.

Article 12

No one shall be subjected to arbitrary interference with his privacy, family, home or correspondence, nor to attacks upon his honour and reputation. Everyone has the right to the protection of the law against such interference or attacks.

Article 13

(1) Everyone has the right to freedom of movement and residence within the borders of each state.

(2) Everyone has the right to leave any country, including his own, and to return to his country.

Article 14

Everyone has the right to seek and to enjoy in other countries asylum from persecution.

Article 15

Everyone has the right to a nationality.

Article 16

Men and women of full age, without any limitation due to race, nationality or religion, have the right to marry and to found a family.

Article 17

Everyone has the right to own property alone as well as in association with others.

Article 18

Everyone has the right to freedom of thought, conscience and religion.

Article 19

Everyone has the right to freedom of opinion and expression.

Article 20

Everyone has the right to freedom of peaceful assembly and association.

Article 21

(1) Everyone has the right to take part in the government of his country, directly or through freely chosen representatives.

(2) Everyone has the right of equal access to public service in his country.

Article 22

Everyone, as a member of society, has the right to social security.

Article 23

(1) Everyone has the right to work, to free choice of employment, to just and favourable conditions of work and to protection against unemployment.

(2) Everyone, without any discrimination, has the right to equal pay for equal work.

(3) Everyone who works has the right to just and favourable remuneration.

(4) Everyone has the right to form and to join trade unions for the protection of his interests.

Article 24

Everyone has the right to rest and leisure, including reasonable limitation of working hours and periodic holidays with pay.

Article 25

Everyone has the right to a standard of living adequate for the health and wellbeing of himself and of his family, including food, clothing, housing and medical care and necessary social services, and the right to security in the event of unemployment, sickness, disability, widowhood, old age or other lack of livelihood in circumstances beyond his control.

Article 26

Everyone has the right to education.

Article 27

(1) Everyone has the right freely to participate in the cultural life of the community, to enjoy the arts and to share in scientific advancement and its benefits.

(2) Everyone has the right to the protection of the moral and material interests resulting from any scientific, literary or artistic production of which he is the author.

Article 28

Everyone is entitled to a social and international order in which the rights and freedoms set forth in this Declaration can be fully realised.

17

8 What can cause problems in communities?

In this lesson you will:
★ consider problems from more than one point of view
★ learn about the importance of talking and negotiating in solving problems
★ look at the role of mediation in problem-solving.

Starter activity

Most people live happily together in their communities but sometimes things go wrong. What sorts of problems can arise between people who live in the same community?

The problems that arise in communities may often have more than one cause. There will be the particular incident or problem that has cropped up but people's underlying feelings can also make a situation more difficult.

For example, if people feel angry, frightened or threatened, they may respond in a way that makes the situation worse.

Source 1

Get Active 1

Look at the photograph in Source 1. It shows a group of young people who regularly gather together on one of the streets of a residential neighbourhood. The girls are sitting on the garden wall of someone's house and the boys are on the pavement on their bikes. Several residents are unhappy about the young people meeting like this.

1 What do you think the residents are concerned about?

2 What feelings might the residents have that might make the situation flare up?

3 How do you think a resolution might be reached?

Anna

You are an enthusiastic amateur gardener keen on self sufficiency and 'green' issues. You rented an allotment earlier this year and are growing your own fruit and veg. You won't use

weedkiller and you work hard to keep your patch clear of weeds. You enjoy the friendly atmosphere between the different allotment holders and look forward to your weekly visits. However, you are concerned that George's weeds are creeping into your plot and killing your plants.

George

Your allotment is next to Anna's. You've had it for years and don't worry too much about weeds and creepers – as long as you can grow flowers and a few seasonal vegetables to take home to the family you are happy. Recently you haven't been able to visit as often as you'd like since your back has started playing up. Things are getting a bit out of hand on your allotment but you don't consider it a big problem.

Jay

You are 14 years old and your parents have split up. You are happy at your present school and have lots of friends there. Your dad and his new partner have moved to the next town – about five miles away. Your mum is staying in the house where you all lived together and wants you to live with her. Your school is half way between both their homes so whatever happens you won't need to move schools. You'd like to spend your time equally with both parents – but they're angry with each other and won't discuss things.

Jon

You are Jay's father. You and your wife have split up after being together for sixteen years. You have had to move out of the home you all shared. You really miss Jay and would like it if Jay came to live with you. You feel really upset about the situation. Your ex-wife is angry with you and won't allow you back in the house. She completely blames you for the breakdown of the relationship. She doesn't want to speak to you.

Niquil

You are the middle child of a family of three children aged nine to fifteen. You live with your dad on the sixth floor of a block of flats in the Derwent Estate. You like to play in the street and to ride your bike on the pavement, where it feels safer than on the road. Your dad is happy for you to play outside until he gets home from work or it gets dark.

Sam

You are retired and live alone in a house with its own garden on the Derwent Estate. You like to go for a walk at least once a day but don't feel as steady on your feet as you used to. You enjoy having families around you, they liven up the neighbourhood, but you are worried about being knocked over by children riding their bikes on the pavement and playing in the street.

Get Active 2

Look at the situations described in Source 2. Working in groups, answer the following questions for one of the situations:

1 What reasonable point could either side raise to explain their concerns?
2 What feelings might each side be experiencing?
3 What negotiations and compromises would be necessary for the characters to achieve an outcome where both feel happier?

Mediation

One way that community or family disputes can be resolved is by a process called 'mediation'. You may already have come across pupil mediation services in school which sometimes deal with issues such as bullying. Here are just three examples of services that can help provide advice and/or mediation when things go wrong:

- Some local councils have a mediation service to resolve disputes between neighbours.

- The Citizen's Advice Bureau can provide useful advice to anyone with a problem.

- Independent mediation services or charities are often used by families who are experiencing problems.

Source 3 Mediation

What is mediation?	How does mediation work?
Mediation is a way of dealing with disputes which helps people to reach an agreement that everybody is satisfied with.	The mediators will listen to what each person has to say and help them explore the options available.
Mediation does not judge or blame people but tries to help people work towards an agreement for the future.	The mediator will not tell the people what to do but will help them reach an agreement.
Mediation helps all the issues to be heard and understood. It may be that some of the people involved do not realise that there is a problem.	

Get Active 3

Look at the information in Source 3. Discuss what situations in school and your other communities might be helped if mediation was available.

Get Active 4

How would you complete this sentence: 'If people aren't listening to each other, mediation is the best policy because …'?

How can I contribute to my community?

In this lesson you will:
* ★ **look at community services and who provides them**
* ★ **consider how volunteers contribute to their communities**
* ★ **think about ways in which you could contribute to your community.**

Starter activity

Your local authority will have an obligation to provide a range of services. Do you know what those services are? Make a class list.

In British communities, services are provided by various groups, for example the local authority (council); Primary Care (health) Trust; police; national charities and agencies such as the Samaritans; local charities and voluntary community groups.

Get Active 1

Here are some problems that a community might face:

* a busy road with no pedestrian crossing
* nowhere for children to play
* an elderly person who is cold and lonely.

Who do you think should put these things right? Explain why it should be up to them to do so.

In British communities, the government ensures that a wide range of services are provided locally. Alongside this, people have built up a strong tradition of voluntary and community support. An example of this is given in Source 1 on page 22, a case study of Aghalee Village Hall in Northern Ireland which won the Queen's Award for Voluntary Service.

Source 1 Aghalee Village Hall

Case study

Aghalee Village Hall Management Committee has run the village hall for over 70 years, providing local residents with a focal point for their social, educational and sporting activities. Every day some activity takes place in the hall, including Tiny Tots Playgroup, a club for the elderly, dog training classes, junior ballet, a junior sports club, a badminton club, local art classes and Alcoholics Anonymous meetings. The local Development Association also hold their monthly meetings in the hall.

The two biggest events that the Management Committee run are the annual Children's Sports and Fun Day, which is followed by a barbeque and dance in the hall; and the annual Lighting of the Christmas Tree with a visit by Father Christmas.

Many community groups pay to use the hall. This income is largely used to pay for the maintenance and upkeep of the hall. On Friday evenings the hall has become increasingly popular for private functions and birthday parties for both the young and old – this is another way of raising funds to keep the hall safe and weather-proof.

Since 1933 the hall has been run by volunteers who are elected at the AGM. The Committee is representative of all the user groups and members of the local community. One of the major concerns of the Committee is to keep the village hall in as good a state of repair as possible in order that it will continue to be appreciated by all the user groups.

(Aghalee Village Hall Management Committee, Lisburn, N. Ireland.)

Get Active 2

Spilt into teams and read the case study in Source 1 above. This is an example of a successful and busy venue supporting and being supported by its local community. Imagine that as part of a local initiative your team have been given a building that comprises a main hall, several meeting rooms, a kitchen, lavatories and grounds around the building that can be used for a variety of activities. The facility has comprehensive disabled access. You need to run this community venue for the benefit of as many different groups as possible. In your teams discuss the following questions:

1 Which groups do you already know about in your community who could use this venue?
2 Using the case study in Source 1 for ideas, what range of activities would you introduce in order to attract other members of the community to use your venue?

People in Aghalee have been running their community venue on a voluntary basis for over 70 years. Think of the thousands of voluntary hours that members of the community have donated to help this project and each other. Opposite are some of the ways in which members of the community contributed their time.

- accounting and running the finances
- cleaning
- cooking and serving meals
- fundraising
- gardening and maintenance of the grounds
- keeping the bookings diary
- keeping the building well maintained and safe
- liaising with the local council
- marketing what the facility offers
- painting and decorating
- running courses/ classes
- secretarial work.

Get Active 3

Look at the list of activities that you generated in Get Active 2 and the list of tasks opposite that the volunteers at Aghalee undertake. In pairs, answer the following questions:

1 Do you think you could help to teach a class or run an activity? What would it be?
2 Which tasks could you contribute to?
3 What qualities do you think you have to offer your community?

While you are still at school it won't necessarily be easy or appropriate to commit a lot of time to volunteering. However, many people your age do contribute to their communities in different ways. For example, Young Voices was a Community Service Volunteers project that aimed to actively involve young people as volunteers within public libraries. It aimed to encourage more young people to use the library, to volunteer in the library and to learn new skills. The project was funded by a grant from the Big Lottery Young People's Fund.

A large number of voluntary organisations have to raise a least a proportion of their own funds and cannot always rely on getting a grant. Hospices are an example of this (see Source 2 below). Help the Hospices is the leading charity supporting hospice care throughout the UK.

Source 2 The Hospice Movement

The vision of the Hospice Movement is that everyone at the end of their life should have access to the best possible care. A quarter of a million patients are cared for by the Hospice Movement in the UK each year, either in a hospice or in their own home.

Over 100,000 people volunteer in hospices across the UK. Without them, hospices could not continue to do the work that they do.

Help the Hospices did a survey in 2006 which found that the financial value of volunteers to hospices was over £112 million. This means that if hospices paid people to do the work done by volunteers, their costs would increase by nearly a quarter.

Hospices are the largest fundraising cause in the UK – they need to raise over £400 million every year to keep going.

Schools could really make a difference to their local hospice. There are several ways they can help, including:

• fundraising
• collecting items for the hospice shops
• helping in the hospice.

Get Active 4

Read Source 2 about the Hospice Movement. This is just one example of a group who needs the support of volunteers. As a class, discuss the following questions:

1 What do you think might be the most effective way of raising funds for the Hospice Movement?
2 How could you undertake this as part of a school project?

Get Active 5

What do you do that makes a positive contribution to your community?

How can we cope with stress?

Starter activity

Stress is sometimes defined as:
constant worry and/or a feeling of tension/anxiety.

● **What does 'stress' mean to you?**
● **How do different people experience it?**
● **What do you think causes it?**

Get Active 1

What simple ways do you know of that a person could use to reduce the stress they are feeling? For example, listening to favourite or relaxing music can help many people. Discuss and list your ideas in pairs.

Source 1 Coping with study stress

✓ Eat well and don't skip breakfast: your body needs energy throughout the day.
✓ Make a revision plan or timetable if you have got a lot on.
✓ Take lots of breaks and reward yourself for reaching reasonable goals.
✓ Revise in the best way for you: everyone has different ways of learning and remembering things.
✓ Explain your study plans to the people you live with so they can understand what you're doing and try to give you the space and quiet you need.
✓ Don't 'cram' the night before a test, do some light revision.
✓ Once all your exams are over get out and have some fun.

Get Active 2

Look at Source 1. Study stress is a common example of stress shared by many of us. Think about a situation that has made you feel stressed in the past. Work in a pair or in a group of four. Remind yourselves of your Group Agreement from Chapter 1 and in particular everyone's right to privacy – you only need to talk about what you want to.

Think about your stressful situation and answer these questions:

1 How did you behave at the time?
2 Could you have behaved differently in the situation, so that you could have felt more in control?
3 If you had acted differently, would it have changed what happened?

Even when we try and develop our own strategies to help us deal with stress, there can be times when we feel overwhelmed by the situation and forget to use them. At times like these, understanding and support from other people can make it much easier to cope. Feeling alone makes it hard. You may find it helpful to ask for support in difficult times, and others may find it helpful to call on you.

Get Active 3

Look at Source 2. Working in pairs, answer one of the letters in order to help the person writing cope with their stressful situation. Remember it may not be possible to solve their problems for them – but you can provide help, guidance and support in your response.

---

1 *My parents are splitting up*
I'm in Year 8 at school and I'm feeling really miserable. I've heard my mum and dad discussing that they don't want to be together any more and one of them is going to move out. I've heard loads of people say that there is so much divorce around that children are used to dealing with it – but I don't feel like that. I'm sacred and I'm unhappy – and I feel completely alone.

2 *Someone I love has died*
Six months ago my aunt died. She was really lovely and I got on with her so well – we could talk about all kinds of things. Both my parents work, so in the school holidays I'd spend a lot of time round at her house. My family were really sad when she died and we cried a lot. Now they don't talk about her so much and I'm worried about telling them how much I miss her in case I upset them again.

3 *My brother is drinking too much*
My older brother Paul drinks every night. He doesn't always go out drinking with his mates - on the nights he's at home he takes the bottles up to his room. It seems like there isn't one night that goes by without him drinking. There's so much on the telly and in the papers about the dangers of alcohol that I'm worried he could get really ill. I don't think it would be right for me to tell on him and I don't know what to say to him about it.

4 *I thought Sam really loved me but I've been dumped*
I've been going out with Sam for three months. It's been brilliant – we spent ages together whenever we were free. I really thought this was the Real Thing and made any excuse I could to be with Sam. Now Sam's dumped me I realise I made a big mistake because whilst we were seeing each other I didn't spend time with my friends. Now I'm alone – in all sorts of ways.

Source 2 Problem page

Get Active 4

Think back over all the different advice for combating stress that has been discussed in this lesson. What single thing should you remember to help you cope with stress in the future?

11 How can we respond under pressure?

In this lesson you will:
★ **remember ways to 'be assertive'**
★ **have the opportunity to experience being confident**
★ **identify strategies to support you when you feel pressurised.**

There are all sorts of things we naturally want to say 'no' to: being told to clean our rooms; doing our regular chores; being told to go to bed when we're doing something else; etc.

On the other hand there are times we might want to say 'no' to something or somebody but find it difficult to do so.

Starter activity

Look at Source 1. The photographs illustrate people who may want to say 'no' to the situation they are in.

● **Do you feel you always have the choice to say no?**
● **In what circumstances is it difficult to say no?**
● **Is it important to be able to say no?**

Source 1

Being able to say 'no' so that people know you mean it is a valuable skill. This is particularly true when it affects our health and/or our safety. In the past you may have looked at ways of being clear and assertive about what you mean. Look at Source 2 – it should remind you.

Source 2

Being assertive – some tips
☐ Sit or stand up straight – your body language should be relaxed but not casual.

☐ Look directly at the person you are talking to.

☐ Use a clear, firm voice.

☐ Say what you want or need.

Get Active 1

Saying no is easier when you feel confident. Think of a time when you felt really good about yourself. Perhaps you finished a piece of work that you'd been finding difficult; maybe somebody told you they were proud of you; or you knew you'd done something good and felt quietly happy inside yourself.

Think about what it would be like to be one of the gold medal winners standing on the podium at the Olympics, or the winner of *X Factor* and be given a record contract. Imagine you are that person. Now that you are visualising what being confident feels like, describe how your chosen situation feels by answering the following questions:

1 What's happening?
2 What things can you see?
3 Can you hear anything in particular?
4 What are you thinking about?
5 How does it feel?

Feeling confident is much easier when we feel we know what is about to happen, and when we feel safe and secure about who we are with and what we are doing. However, we can't always expect to be in that safe situation. We need to practise for the unexpected times when things might go wrong and we may want to refuse to do what someone asks of us. Saying no may mean we hurt someone's feelings.

Get Active 2

Sometimes we may feel others put pressure on us to do something we don't want to do or to go along with something we don't feel comfortable with. Look at Source 3 on the right. Working in pairs, come up with a way that Pupil B could respond to each thing Pupil A says in order to refuse the request and still stay friends.

Get Active 3

Here are some other situations where a young person might want or need to say no:

- at a party where a group of friends is drinking a lot of alcohol
- at the shopping mall where a group dare each other to shoplift
- on the way home from school where a group decide to kick around the bag of a younger pupil
- on public transport where a group barge past the queue
- in the park where a group decide to skate on a frozen pond.

Choose one of these situations and work with a partner to create a dialogue between the person who wants to say no and another member of the group who is encouraging them to take part. Your aim is to try and reach a solution that enables the person to refuse whilst still remaining part of the group.

Get Active 4

Identify one step from today's lesson that could help you cope in a situation where you feel pressured.

Source 3

12 What's the right balance between work and leisure?

In this lesson you will:
★ **consider what the phrase 'a healthy balance' means**
★ **apply the idea of 'a healthy balance' to your own situation**
★ **use a problem-solving approach to achieving solutions.**

Starter activity

How can people keep themselves healthy? List as many ideas as you can in one minute.

Individuals can do many things to look after their own health. Each of us is responsible for taking steps to look after ourselves. This isn't just about our physical health but also about balancing our emotions and our relationships with other people.

How does the idea of 'a healthy balance' apply to your life? The phrase 'a healthy balance' can be applied to all sorts of things – eating a variety of foods; undertaking a range of activities – some of which may be physical and some of which might be couch or desk based. You will already know that getting enough sleep is as important as taking regular exercise.

Source 1
Time wheel

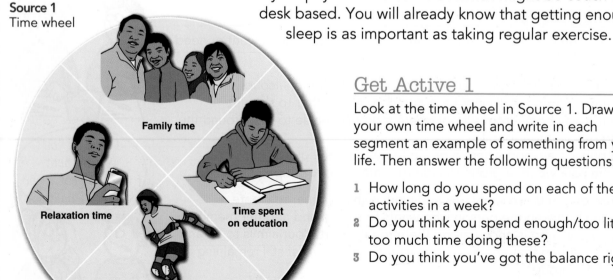

Family time

Relaxation time

Activity time

Time spent on education

Get Active 1

Look at the time wheel in Source 1. Draw your own time wheel and write in each segment an example of something from your life. Then answer the following questions:

1 How long do you spend on each of these activities in a week?
2 Do you think you spend enough/too little/too much time doing these?
3 Do you think you've got the balance right?

Balance isn't necessarily something that is measured out in equal amounts. Different people in your life will have different views on what a healthy balance might be between enjoying free time and getting your tasks done.

Source 2
What's the problem?

a)
b)
c)
d)

Get Active 2

Look at the 'situations' in Source 2 which show family disagreements about enjoying free time and getting tasks done. In groups, decide what the different characters are saying for one of the situations and list some points to explain each character's point of view.

As we have seen, disagreements between parents and children are often about how much time is spent on tasks as opposed to leisure. If families communicated better with each other there would probably be less conflict or disagreement amongst family members. A good way for families to handle difficult situations is through problem-solving. This means talking over the situation and arriving at a solution that is fair and acceptable to all involved. Each person in a family will need to remember that we should consider each other's feelings and viewpoints even when we disagree.

Get Active 3

Look at Source 3. This four stage solution is one way in which family disagreements can be resolved. In groups, apply the four stage solution to one of the situations in Source 2 and write down the answer to each stage in turn.

Get Active 4

'When I was a boy of 14, my father was so ignorant I could hardly stand to have the old man around. But when I got to be 21, I was astonished at how much the old man had learned in seven years.'

Mark Twain – author of *Huckleberry Finn* and *The Adventures of Tom Sawyer*.

What point do you think Mark Twain was making?

Source 3

> **Problem to solution in four stages**
>
> Stage 1: What's the problem?
>
> Stage 2: What are the possible ways of solving the problem?
>
> Stage 3: Of the possible ways, which ones best solve the problem?
>
> Stage 4: Which solution provides the best balance for everyone?

Am I a streetwise shopper?

In this lesson you will:
* ★ **learn how to complain and exercise your rights when purchasing products**
* ★ **find out about consumer rights and the Sale of Goods Act.**

Starter activity

Shopping is something people often feel extreme emotions about – they either love it or hate it. Look at Source 1 – what feelings do the photos suggest to you?

Source 1 Experiences when shopping

When we are looking for something we want for ourselves then shopping doesn't seem like a chore – but if it's the weekly trip to the supermarket or buying new school uniform then it's probably the last thing we would choose to do.

When we are very young our parents or carers have to shop for us. As we get older we shop with them – sometimes we choose and they pay!

Get Active 1

1 What things do you shop for on your own and what do you shop for with your parents or carers?
2 Have you ever bought something that has gone wrong or been faulty? What did you do?

Imagine you drop a brand new iPod and it breaks. Does the shop have to do anything to help you? In fact, they don't – people can only get repairs, replacements or their money back if they have not done anything to make the item break or cause damage to it themselves.

When you have to take goods back to a shop, sometimes the salesperson can be very helpful and sometimes they may seem unwilling to help.

Get Active 2

Now imagine you have bought an iPod which stops working after two days. You know you have followed the instructions completely and now you are feeling pretty fed up. Work with another person to script a conversation between you and the salesperson. You want your money back or a replacement – what are the 'dos and don'ts' of how to go about this?

You are likely to be shopping more independently at your age; therefore it is important to gain some understanding of shopping safety:

- be aware that buying something that is faulty can be a real problem
- you must prove that the fault wasn't caused by yourself
- you must prove that you bought it from that shop
- you should return it in a certain amount of time that helps your case, and ideally as soon as possible
- you need to deal with the situation with as little stress as possible.

Knowing your consumer rights will help you to deal with situations in the most effective way:

- check goods before you buy them
- ask what the shop's refund policy is
- always ask for a receipt
- buy from reputable traders
- the Sale of Goods Act says that, if you realise that what you have bought is faulty or not of the quality you would expect from something brand new, then you are entitled to a full refund or an exchange of the item(s)
- you should return faulty goods as soon as possible; a shop may argue that it is wear and tear or your fault if you leave it too long.

Get Active 3

Look at Source 2 on the right and the advice on shopping above. Work together in a small group to answer the following questions about each picture:

1 What is the problem?
2 Should Karen complain to the shop she bought the item from?
3 What are Karen's rights as a consumer?
4 What if Karen complains and the people in the shop will not listen?
5 What should Karen do next?

Get Active 4

Invent a slogan for 'Streetwise Shoppers Week' that incorporates one piece of good advice that you have learnt in this lesson.

Source 2 Karen the Consumer

A Karen is in a hurry when she buys her skirt and doesn't take advantage of the changing room provided to try it on. When she gets home she finds it is too small.

B Karen bought a new laptop last week. When she sits down to do her homework and turns on the power it suddenly bursts into flames. She burns her hand.

14 Am I an ethical consumer?

> **In this lesson you will:**
> ★ **identify some of the influences on you as a consumer**
> ★ **learn about 'ethical consumerism'**
> ★ **apply ideas about ethical consumerism to your community.**

We all make decisions (conscious or subconscious) about the way in which we buy goods and services. Many factors affect the decisions that we make.

Starter activity

Look at the photographs below. They give some different ideas about what influences how, why and where you shop for clothes. Brainstorm a list of influences, including the ideas given in the photos and those of your own.

Source 1
Shopping ethically means buying products which were produced according to a set of values – as the examples in these photographs show.

There are many factors that may influence our decisions if we actually stop and think about them. You may have heard the expression 'ethical shopping'. What does this mean?

Human rights being met – good working conditions

Recycled Paper

Environmental sustainability – wood from a renewable source

Animal welfare – free-range chickens

Ethical profit sharing – buying 'fair trade' goods

Ethical shopping can be as simple as buying free-range eggs or as complex as boycotting goods produced by child labour. Examples of products that commonly fall into the 'ethical category' include fair trade goods, recycled paper and wood products from managed forests, electric cars and cosmetics not tested on animals.

Get Active 1

Look at Source 1 opposite. It shows some of the values that affect how we choose to shop ethically. For each one, give an example of a situation where these ethical values might be ignored or overlooked when shopping and why. An example is given on the right.

Get Active 2

Being a consumer isn't only about shopping – it is also about the way we use goods and services. In groups, make a list of ways that your community could reduce wasteful use of utility services such as electricity, gas, water, etc.

There are many practices that we may consider to be ethically wrong but actually know very little about. Overall, ethical spending is still a small proportion of the total annual consumer spend; however, awareness of ethical issues is increasing.

> Example:
> Animal welfare – egg-producing chickens are sometimes kept in overcrowded conditions with no daylight or room to move but people choose to buy eggs that are not free-range because they are cheaper.

Get Active 3

Look at Source 2. In this report, ethical spending appears to have increased in all areas except travel and transport.

1 Why do you think there was no change in the area of greener travel and transport?
2 What could the local and national government do to encourage people to make greener choices when it comes to travel and transport?

Many organisations provide information on consumer issues which enable individuals to act ethically when making their decisions about purchasing. You might want to explore these further to help you in your purchasing decisions. Some places to start are:

- www.tradingstandards.gov.uk
- www.getethical.com
- www.ethicalconsumer.org

Get Active 4

In order to start becoming a more ethical consumer, what one thing could you change today about the way you shop or use services?

Trends in ethical consumerism

In the 12 months from November 2007–November 2008 …

Spending on ethical food and drink, which includes organic products, fair trade goods and free-range eggs, was up 14 per cent.

Green home expenditure, which incorporates energy-efficient electrical appliances, green mortgage repayments, small renewables (such as micro-wind turbines) and green energy, was up 13 per cent.

Spending on personal products, such as humane cosmetics and eco-fashion (e.g. fair trade cotton), was up 4 per cent.

Monies in ethical finance, which includes ethical banking and investments, was up 15 per cent.

Eco-travel and transport costs including environmentally friendly transport, responsible tour operators, public transport and sales of 'green cars' didn't change.

Source 2

How enterprising am I? Part 1

In this lesson you will:
- ★ learn about the concept of 'enterprise' and how this works
- ★ work with others to practise the skills of creating a new business
- ★ consider a range of economic ideas, for example limiting risk.

Some of you may have watched the TV programme *Dragons' Den*. You may not know that it was first launched on television in Japan. *Dragons' Den* is now an international brand with versions airing in countries across the globe. In the programme members of the public with ideas for new business ventures pitch for investment in the Den from the Dragons. These members of the public are 'enterprising' people, that is, they have used their creativity to develop new business ideas. The Dragons are business people who are willing to invest their own money in exchange for a share of the new business.

Source 1 Two enterprising and successful people who pitched in the *Dragons' Den*

Name:
Sharon Wright

Pitching:
Magnamole

Investment required:
£80,000

Investment secured:
£80,000 for 22.5% of the company

Brief description: An invention that threads cables through cavity walls using magnets

Name:
Levi Roots

Pitching:
Reggae Reggae Sauce

Investment required:
£50,000 for 20%

Investment secured:
£50,000 for 40% of the company

Brief description: Hot spicy barbecue sauce and seasonings

Starter activity

Look at Source 1 above. It shows two enterprising and successful people who pitched in the *Dragons' Den* with two very different products. Have you ever wanted to invent anything? Work with another person to share your ideas.

Finding innovative and successful new products and services isn't always easy. A good way to get started is to decide on your 'target group' and then identify what services and products they might wish to buy.

Get Active 1

This exercise will help you formulate ideas for a new business. Look at Source 2, which shows working mothers as a target group.

- Copy the hexagon outline onto a large sheet of paper.
- Choose a new target group (for example, teenage girls, toddlers, retired people, etc.) and write it in the centre of your diagram.
- You will need to think about the lifestyle of this new group and add these aspects to your diagram.
- For each lifestyle aspect, show the products and services that the people in your target market would find useful. How could these be developed into a new business idea?

Get Active 2

Now that you have an idea for a business you need to write a business plan. An example of a business plan is given in Source 3. This will show potential investors that the business is worth investing in. In the *Dragons' Den* it is the product and the business plan together that form the 'pitch'.

Get Active 3

Now that you have your product/service and business plan ready, you need to devise a pitch for funds to start running your business. Prepare a pitch that lasts no more than two minutes. You can use a variety of media. When completed you will present your pitch to the rest of the class.

Get Active 4

Take a vote as a whole class: which was the product that was most worth funding and why?

Source 2 Business ideas

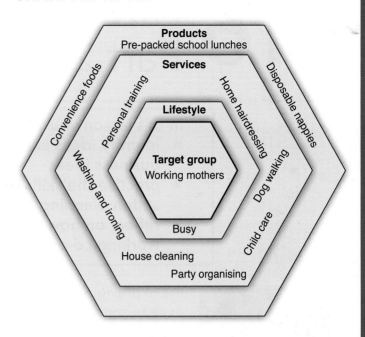

Source 3 A business plan

BUSINESS PLAN
Business name:
What will your business be called?
Business idea:
What is the product or service?   What is its potential to be successful?   What competition will there be from others?   How do you limit the risks involved?   How will the product/service be promoted?   What will you charge?
Target market:
Whom is the product/service aimed at?   Why are these customers likely to buy it?
Finance:
What will you need money for?   Where might you get this money?

16 How enterprising am I? Part 2

In this lesson you will:
★ **identify ideas and methods to promote new business ideas**
★ **practise the skills of problem-solving and action planning**
★ **reflect on how successful your group was in working co-operatively.**

Lord Alan Sugar

In the previous lesson, *Dragons' Den* was used as a model to explore some ideas about business planning. This lesson uses ideas from *The Apprentice* – a series which sets its candidates a series of challenging tasks. One of the challenges in each series is to devise an effective advertising campaign to launch a new product or service. Groups work in teams and nominate a project manager who is responsible for leading the task.

At the end of the task, the candidates are called to the boardroom. The team with the most successful campaign wins.

Starter activity

Look back to the previous lesson at the list of possible businesses (products/services) that your class thought would have been worth funding. Identify one idea that you think would help promote each product or service to potential customers.

Get Active 1

Working in groups, choose one of the products or services from the previous lesson that you thought were worth funding and devise an advertising plan for promoting this product/service. Use Source 1 opposite as a guide. Remember to choose a good name for your product or business.

Get Active 2

Now that you have your advertising plan, in your groups design and prepare the advert itself. You will need to ensure that you follow the plan closely. Remember to put your USP (unique selling point) across to your audience effectively.

Check your finished advert to ensure it meets all the criteria you set out in your plan.

Source 1 Planning an advert to promote your product in a magazine (or other form of print)

1 Choose the name of your product.

2 Define the USP (unique selling point) of your product – this should be the main message of the advert.

3 Know your target audience – what style of advert will appeal to them most? For example, a younger audience might be drawn to a 'busy' advert with lots of images and different fonts.

4 Choose the images that you want to appear in your advert – will they be of the product or of something else?

5 Decide where the images and text should go.

This advert clearly shows the product and its range

This advert doesn't show the product (Ready Brek) but relies on the consumer recognising the brand from the images being used

Get Active 3

This lesson has been about advertising, but in fact it has also encouraged you to develop your group work skills. Look at Source 2 below. Read the questions carefully on your own and give each section a score.

Source 2 Self-assessment chart

	SUCCESSFUL GROUP WORK QUALITIES	HOW DID WE DO? Questions to ask ourselves	SELF-ASSESSMENT: score out of 5 5 = excellent 1 = poor
WORKING TOGETHER	• Doing my best • Helping others to do their best • Not giving up	• How much did team members encourage each other? • Did the team give up?	
MOTIVATION	• Using good communication skills • Being supportive of each other all the time • Using lots of different skills	• Did we listen to each other? • Did we discuss how to share the tasks? • Did we remain supportive throughout?	
THINKING	• Being creative • Trying new ideas	• Did we discuss various answers and solutions? • Did we offer any new ideas?	
COMPLETING THE TASK	• Seeing it through to the end • Keeping focused on the task • Everyone participating	• Did we complete the task on time? • Did we complete the task successfully? • Did everyone contribute?	

17 How do my choices about education affect my financial future?

In this lesson you will:
★ identify some of the implications of staying in full-time education
★ consider the pros and cons of further education or employment
★ learn about some of the financial products available to support future study.

Starter activity

Imagine you need to raise £50 in the next three months. What enterprising ideas do you have that are honest and legal and do not involve simply asking an adult for money?

Until you are 17 your parents/carers have a responsibility to keep you in full-time education. The school leaving age has altered quite a bit over the years (see Source 1).

Source 1 Raising the school leaving age

1880	Minimum school leaving age is fixed at 10 years
1893	Minimum leaving age raised to 11
1899	Minimum leaving age raised to 12
1918	Minimum leaving age raised to 14
1939	Minimum leaving age was to be raised to 15 but it was not implemented because of Second World War
1947	Minimum leaving age raised to 15
1959–1971	Lots of debate which eventually led to …
1972	Minimum leaving age raised to 16
2008	Minimum leaving age raised to 17 for pupils starting Year 7 in that year

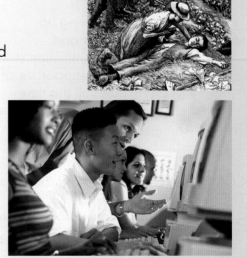

Get Active 1

Look at Source 1 opposite. The school leaving age has steadily risen over the last 120 years which means that you now have to stay at school until you are at least 17 – giving you the education or training you need to earn your own income. If you have older brothers of sisters they may have left school when they were 16. What difference will waiting to 17 instead of 16 make to you?

Get Active 2

In Year 9 you will consider your study options for Key Stage 4. When you are 17 you will have another set of options opening up to you. Look at Source 2 on the right. What are the pros and cons of each choice?

Get Active 3

If you decide to continue studying beyond 17 and go into higher education, you will need to think about the financial implications for yourself and your family. How can you help your parents/carers if they continue to support you financially?

Source 3 Higher education – financial pathways open to you

Source 2 Choices to make at 17

Go to work full time

Continue studying for further qualifications at school or college

Join an apprenticeship scheme (from the age of 16 onwards)

A student loan

Student loans from the government are there to help with the costs of higher education. If you're an eligible full-time student you'll be able to take out two student loans for each year of your course: a loan for tuition fees to cover your fees in full, and a loan for maintenance to help with your accommodation and other living costs.

A bursary

A bursary is non-repayable support available to a wide range of students. Bursaries and scholarships are extra sources of financial help available from colleges and universities. They're paid on top of any student loans or grants you may get.

A grant

A grant is an amount of money which you may qualify for, depending on your circumstances. The government provide grants; other grants may be available from charitable bodies and trusts.

Get Active 4

1 Look at Source 3. Imagine you decided to continue your studies – consider how you would complete these statements:

- In the future I want to study …
- I will get money to help me do this by …
- I will seek advice about financing my future study from …

2 What other facts do you know, or can find out, about financial pathways?

Get Active 5

What advice would you give to somebody who faced leaving school aged 17, with no qualifications?

How do I manage my feelings?

In this lesson you will learn to:
★ **recognise a range of strong emotions that affect how we feel**
★ **consider how strong or negative feelings can be managed**
★ **think about the concept of 'resilience'.**

Fraser's story

Fraser is 15 years old and lives with his mum. This morning at breakfast she checked he'd done all his homework because recently he'd been late with several assignments. His mum soon realised that Fraser had not completed his maths. She was absolutely furious and Fraser had never heard her shout so much. She made him sit down and do it at the breakfast table.

Fraser left for school and asked his best mate Simon if he could see his homework. Simon said, 'No, you're always borrowing it.'

At school he saw Sindy and asked her the same question. Sindy showed him her homework and their answers were virtually the same.

Fraser and Sindy made their way to the maths lesson and found a supply teacher standing in the room – their usual teacher was off sick.

Starter activity

Read Fraser's story above and think about all the different emotions he might have felt from the moment he woke up that morning to the start of his maths lesson. Based on what you've read about Fraser, list as many feelings as you can.

If a relationship is important to us it creates in us all sorts of strong feelings – both positive and negative ones. In Fraser's case, whilst he knows his mum really loves him, he felt very hurt and upset when she lost her temper with him. These strong feelings apply whether the relationship is within your family or with friends: when someone is important to you the feelings matter.

Get Active 1

What feelings have you experienced over friendships you've had in your life? Look at Source 1 and write down those you have experienced.

Although we all experience a range of emotions it does sometimes feel as if they are happening *to* us and we are not in control of our feelings. When this happens it can be tempting to blame other people for how we feel. Blaming other people doesn't actually change anything – what we need to do is deal with our feelings in positive ways that help us get back on track.

Source 1
A field of feelings

happy   jealous   excited

worried   ANTICIPATORY   embarrassed

reassured   *spiteful*   APPRECIATED

loved   *faithful*   relaxed   loyal

respected   impressed

sociable   *fantastic*   outraged

TRUSTED   threatened   PRESSURED

RIDICULED   reliable   UNWANTED

criticised   irrepressible   *irritated*

competitive   *ignored*   carefree

Source 2 How are they feeling?

1: Maalik

Maalik and Christopher met at nursery school. They went up to primary school together and then secondary too. They have been best friends for as long as they can both remember. Christopher's dad, Jeff, has been commuting long distances in his new job for the past year. The family have decided that when Christopher reaches the end of Year 9 they will move to a new home situated near to where Jeff now works. It will be a move that takes them 250 miles away.

Maalik knows that entering Year 10 and working towards his GCSEs is going to be really challenging and on top of that his best friend is moving away.

2: Kira

Kira's parents have just told her that this year's Easter holiday will include a visit to Disneyland, Paris. This will be the first time she's travelled abroad and she can't wait to tell her friends about it.

When she meets up with her friends Kira tells them all about her family's plans. Emily says, 'It's alright – I've been there before, loads of times … This year we're off to Disneyworld in Florida for the whole Easter break … and then we're going swimming with dolphins.'

3: Cody and Casey

Cody and Casey usually spend Saturdays together. This week Cody suggests to Casey that they visit the new leisure park and try out the bowling alley and some of the other stuff there. Casey says that he can't go because he's already promised his mum that he'll stay home to help strip the wallpaper ready for his room to be re-decorated.

Cody decides she'll go to the leisure park anyway and on her way there she sees Casey walking into the park with Barry who is one of his other mates – they've got a football with them.

Get Active 2

Read Source 2. Working in small groups, discuss one of the scenarios and answer these questions:

1 How might the character in the title of your scenario be feeling?
2 Who might they want to blame for how they're feeling?
3 What help and advice would you give them to deal with their feelings in a positive way?

www.youngminds.org.uk has some good advice to help you look after your emotional health and help you to deal with any difficulties that may arise. Their 'top tips' for staying emotionally healthy are:

- Believe in yourself – be proud of who you are and what you have achieved. We all learn at different paces and excel in some subjects more than others.

- Don't be afraid to ask for help if you need it. No one can cope on their own; we all need help and advice from family, friends and adults working to help young people.

- Take one step at a time – don't feel pressurised into making decisions.

- Looking after your body by getting enough sleep, eating good food and taking exercise can help to promote a healthy mind.

What is resilience?

Why is it that some people bounce back after being hit by life's problems, whilst others find it hard to pick themselves up off the floor? Think back to some of the big challenges in your life: your first day at school; establishing friendships; your performance for the sports team; your role in the Christmas pantomime; sitting tests and exams; moving up to secondary school. We've all made mistakes in some or all of these areas, but those who bounce back, dust themselves off and start all over again are the ones with resilience.

Get Active 3

Look at the example in Source 3. It shows how one person rates their own resilience. For example, they think they are not good at staying positive and optimistic but they do feel able to talk and seek help. Construct your own chart or table which helps you recognise how resilient you are.

Source 3
How resilient am I?

When things go wrong I ...	Not great	OK	Good	Excellent
take personal responsibility		✔		
am skilled at solving my own problems			✔	
stay positive and optimistic	✔			
am able to talk about it and seek help			✔	

Is there a secret to being positive and happy? Not really. But there are definitely things you can do to cultivate a more positive attitude. For a start you can accept that happiness is a choice. When something upsets us, there's a split-second when we can opt to be miserable about it, or not. Of course, this doesn't apply when something deeply upsetting happens but even then people can develop an ability to view things in a more positive light over time.

Get Active 4

If you were to develop one new coping strategy that would enable you to build up your resilience what would it be?

Is anybody perfect?

In this lesson you will:
★ look at what influences the way we feel about ourselves
★ reflect on how people can overcome negative feelings
★ think about how people build the resilience they need.

Sometimes dolls like these are accused of making children and young people feel they can never live up to having the perfect body.
What do you think?

Get Active 1

1 On your own, draw a quick picture of yourself and then label on the picture the things you like about yourself and the things you are less than happy with. Which parts, if any, would you like to change?
2 In pairs, discuss which influences make us unhappy with the way we feel about ourselves – in the way we look or in other ways. For example, do we compare ourselves with images of models in magazines?

There are times when people are made to feel that they are not as good as the people around them. Allan Ahlberg, who wrote Source 1, has tried to express this feeling in his poem.

When we pick teams in the playground,
Whatever the game might be,
There's always somebody left till last
And usually it's me.

I stand there looking hopeful
And tapping myself on the chest,
But the captains pick the others first,
Starting, of course, with the best.

Maybe if teams were sometimes picked
Starting with the worst,
Once in his life a boy like me
Could end up being first!

Source 1 'Picking Teams', by Allan Ahlberg, 1983

Get Active 2

Read Source 1 and, in pairs, answer the following questions:

1 Why do you think it was important for Allan Ahlberg to write this poem?
2 What other situations might leave someone feeling this way?
3 What could a person do to help them overcome the feeling that they are not as good as others?

Jessica Lee, 17

Growing up, I'd watched these American TV shows such as *Sabrina the Teenage Witch* and *Saved by the Bell*. In these programmes, there were schools and I kind of presumed that this is what my school would be like … Before I started senior school, I think that I was looking forward to being a mature adult and meeting new friends and new teachers. Even though I was excited about meeting new people, I was quite worried about it as well as I have Apert's Syndrome which affects the face, hands and feet and so was worried about the other pupils' reaction to this.

… One of the responses that I use even now if someone asks about my hands is, 'oh gosh when did that happen?!' It makes them laugh and makes me feel at ease … The best advice that I could give you: if when you start senior school you are unhappy always tell a teacher and nine times out of ten they'll be able to help. The other piece of advice is just go in and be yourself – because if you're yourself then you can hold your head high and say that you're not trying to be someone different – and believe me people will like you for you!

This is what happened to me – I learnt the hard way as I went through various phases trying to be someone that I wasn't and it didn't work out. In the end I decided to be myself and I have got a lot more friends because of it.

Extract from www.iface.org.uk, a website set up by the Changing Faces charity. This site is for young people aged 11–21 to discuss disfigurement, give and get advice and share personal stories.

Tanni Grey Thompson speaks on the topics of motivation, diversity and achievement. She is the author of *Seize the Day* and *Aim High*. For the past 22 years she has been an athlete. She talks about her feelings when she had to make the decision about using a wheelchair:

The last year I was walking was very difficult and I struggled to hold my body weight through my legs. I fell over a lot. I couldn't run round and play with my friends and then for me having a wheelchair gave me the freedom I wanted … But other people around me saw it as something that was very negative … When I was young … 'giving up' was how it was termed. Using a wheelchair was really bad but for me it was completely the opposite. Having a wheelchair … gave me my freedom.

Actually I've won eleven Paralympic gold medals; I broke thirty-five world records and I've attended five Paralympic games. So, over a twenty-two year period … that's OK!

Baroness Tanni Grey Thompson, DBE

Source 2 Case studies (continued)

Professor Maya Angelou

Maya Angelou is a writer and poet and in her life has been a dancer, composer, singer, teacher, actress, black activist and film maker. Her most famous book is *I Know Why the Caged Bird Sings*.

In an interview Angelou talks about being black and female and six feet tall when she would rather have been 'pretty' or petite because 'everyone seemed to love those girls'. She talks about how she overcame her negative feelings:

If you're black and every model of beauty is either white or dark-skinned black, then it has to create some insecurity in a person like me, who couldn't possibly conform …

I reached into my race memories to find those positive things that I could use to help myself and raise my son. I rejected those things that were negative; and not just the negative from the white community, but the negative from the black community as well. I still reject both of them. I want no part of them …

One of the first things that a young person must internalise, deep down in the blood and bones, is the understanding that although he may encounter many defeats, he must not be defeated …

Look at a diamond: it is the result of extreme pressure. Less pressure, it is crystal; less than that, it's coal; and less than that, it is fossilised leaves or just plain dirt.

Extract from *Conversations with Maya Angelou* by Jeffrey Elliot.

Get Active 3

Read the three case studies in Source 2 (pages 44–5).

1 What experiences are the speakers describing that could have left them feeling they didn't fit in?
2 What ideas and thoughts did they have and how did they behave to help them overcome the difficulties they faced?
3 'You may not control all the events that happen to you but you can decide not to be reduced by them.' How does this quote apply to the people you've just read about?

Get Active 4

Many products and shops have phrases, known as slogans or straplines, which have positive associations, for example:

- 'Every little helps'
- 'Because you're worth it'
- 'Just do it'

What is it about yourself that you like and admire? Write your own strapline to sum you up.

20 What happens when relationships break down?

> **In this lesson you will:**
> ★ **understand that all families experience highs and lows**
> ★ **consider strategies for coping when there are family arguments**
> ★ **look at some of the issues affecting young people in troubled families.**

Source 1
Extract from 'It's All Relative' by Patrick Tolan

Family should mean that arguments can be forgotten
Family should be there when you're feeling downtrodden
Mothers should kiss the wounds that life deals
Fathers should offer advice like no other man can ...

Unfortunately families, like most ideals, are never truly perfected
But this brute fact is not a curse but a blessing
We need our families to be imperfect, that we may experience but a small part of the conflict the world bears
So families need not be any of these things, all they need be ...
... Is Family

Starter activity

Read Source 1. Everyone probably wishes they had the perfect family, but the poet in Source 1 recognises that there is no such thing as perfection where families are concerned. What things happen in reality that can cause problems in family life?

Parents have the right to expect you to behave yourself, do your homework and do your jobs around the house. Not getting the latest designer gear isn't being bullied or neglected!

Sometimes the normal rows between siblings and other family members get heavy. People around you may think your feelings don't need to be taken seriously. They may have so much on their minds they can't see your problem.

Source 2
When it all gets too much

Get Active 1

1 Look at Source 2 opposite. What do you think the young person is:
    • feeling?
    • thinking?
2 What strategies could you suggest to them to help them cope with what is going on?

For some people problems become too complicated for them to deal with on their own. Their best move is to tell a teacher or some other adult they like and trust.

www.there4me.com is a useful place to read more about this if you know someone in this situation.

Sometimes relationships between the parents in a family break down so irretrievably that they decide to split up. Nothing prepares a young person for the break-up of their parents' relationship. Even if they are used to hearing their parents rowing or seeing them ignoring each other, it still comes as a big shock.

The young person may feel totally confused, or it could be a relief if the marriage had been very unhappy. Whatever the cause of the break-up, it is not the young person's fault. They did not cause it and they cannot mend it.

Alex

Alex is aware of the difficulties in his parents' marriage. Both of Alex's parents are unhappy and all their attention and time seems to be spent on dealing with the problems between them. Alex is feeling very distressed, full of negative feelings and fears that need to be expressed, but he is worried that his parents have enough to cope with.

Source 3

Get Active 2

Read Source 3. What advice can you give Alex? Write a script where Alex starts a conversation with his mum and dad. Try to find words that express Alex's feelings.

Within any relationship, there are ups and downs – people say and do things to each other that are hurtful. However, there's a difference between a normal argument and abusive, violent or threatening behaviour. Sometimes disagreements at home turn from arguments to attacks – verbal or physical. This is sometimes referred to as domestic violence or domestic abuse. It can take many forms.

Get Active 3

Read the information sheet that your teacher will give you. In pairs, create an A5-sized flier called 'Personal Help and Information' which has three key messages to encourage and support a young person who may be experiencing domestic violence in their home.

If you are worried about domestic abuse (for yourself or for someone else) you might find it helpful to talk to another adult or one of your teachers about this. Alternatively you can read more and find further help at www.thehideout.org.uk/over10/whatisabuse/default.aspa.

Experiencing ups and downs in family life is normal. Remember: despite what we might see on television or read about in newspapers, the problems in most families do not involve abuse or violence.

Get Active 4

This lesson began with a poem. Write your own three line poem (it can be a haiku) that expresses something positive about your family or a family member.

21 How do we cope with loss and bereavement?

In this lesson you will:
★ explore what 'loss' and 'bereavement' might mean
★ consider ways that people may cope with loss
★ discuss different ways of dealing with death.

Starter activity

When we hear the phrase 'loss and bereavement' many of us naturally think first of death – either of someone we love or of someone we know who is feeling grief because someone they love has died. What other events in our lives might make us feel a sense of loss and painful sadness at missing someone or something?

Now that you are in Year 9 you will have experienced a range of people in your life: a best friend or friends; a very close group of friends that you hang out with; long-standing friends from aspects of your life not connected with school; perhaps a boyfriend or girlfriend. Sometimes those relationships can break down or end suddenly. When this happens you may feel rejected, or sad, or that you can't trust anyone ever again.

Source 1

Anya's feelings

I'm going to be 16 next term. Three months ago Daniel, who I'd been going out with for over a year, suddenly said he was ending our relationship. He didn't give a reason, he just wanted out. The trouble is I just can't seem to get over him. I think of Daniel all the time and keep remembering all the great times we had together. I can't believe how much it hurts – I still keep bursting into tears. I don't think I'll ever be able to trust anyone again.

Freddie's feelings

I'm 15 and play street hockey with my local youth club. We've been doing really well and I made it onto the team that is touring some Dutch youth clubs this summer. It's a great team and I was really looking forward to the tour. Now it's all gone wrong! I broke my ankle at the weekend and I'm going to have to be replaced on the tour. I'm totally fed up. I know the team will have a brilliant time and I won't be part of it. By the time they get back I won't really be part of their group any more. I'm feeling like an outsider already and don't think I even want to go and see them off.

Get Active 1

Read about how Anya and Freddie are feeling in Source 1. In pairs, choose one of them to respond to with some ideas that will help them to cope with their feelings of loss and move forward positively.

All loss can be painful to us but for many people the death of somebody they love is one of the most difficult things they may experience.

Source 2
Prince William in a speech to the Child Bereavement Charity of which he is the royal patron, March 2009

... what I understand now, is that losing a close family member is one of the hardest experiences that anyone can ever endure. Never being able to say the word 'mummy' again in your life sounds like a small thing. However, for many, including me, it is now really just a word – hollow and evoking only memories. I can therefore wholeheartedly relate to the Mother's Day Campaign as I too have felt – and still feel – the emptiness on such a day as Mother's Day.

Get Active 2

Read Source 2 above and discuss the following questions:

1 Is it helpful to hear famous people talk about their grief?
2 Does hearing famous people speak about grief make it OK for us to talk more openly?
3 If you were experiencing a strong sense of loss and grief what do you think would make it easier for you to cope?

Get Active 3

Read Source 3 on the right and discuss the following questions:

1 Do you think Sarah was too young to go her grandfather's funeral?
2 What are the arguments for and against letting children attend funerals?
3 Who should make the final decision about going to a funeral – the child or their parents/carers?

Get Active 4

'Grief shouldn't be swept under the carpet ... grief needs to be brought out into the open, doesn't it?' – spoken by a teenager whose dad had died.

What do you think could be done in school to help someone who is grieving?

Source 3

My grandfather died when I was 11. He lived with us for the last two years of his life and I was very close to him. My parents decided they wouldn't let me go to the funeral; they thought I was too young.

Sarah

I was nine when Auntie Liz died. I'm proud that I went to the funeral service and crematorium.

James

What if I don't want to?

In this lesson you will:
★ remind yourself of a strategy to help you make choices
★ use the strategy to help you advise others
★ think about issues surrounding 'early sex'.

Starter activity

Think back to a time when you were worried about saying no to someone and ended up doing something you didn't want to do. For example, perhaps you lent someone your homework to copy.

One of the reasons people often find it hard to say no is because they don't want to hurt the feelings of a person they care about. This can be particularly true if the other person is someone we feel attracted to and 'fancy' or 'love'. However much we love or care about another person we still have the right to make our own decisions and follow our own choices.

If you followed this PSHE education course in Year 7 you might remember the following four steps – they help you choose what's right for you.

Source 1 The Four Cs

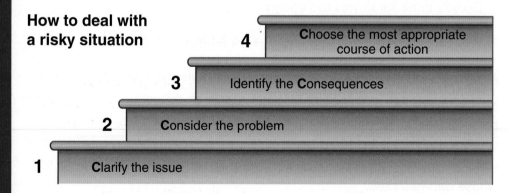

How to deal with a risky situation

4 — Choose the most appropriate course of action

3 — Identify the **C**onsequences

2 — **C**onsider the problem

1 — **C**larify the issue

Get Active 1

Look at the four situations in Source 2 opposite. Choose one situation and use the Four Cs method from Source 1 above to help resolve the problem for the main character. If possible try and achieve a positive outcome for everyone in the situation.

Source 2

1 Galina

Galina is 15. She has known Si who's 16 and part of her crowd for a couple of years. Last time they were all together Si asked her out on her own. Galina was really happy. At the end of the evening Si took Galina back to her house and whilst they were sitting on the couch he snogged her – it felt brilliant. Si then tried to go further … Galina doesn't want to fall out with him – she's known him ages – but she isn't sure she's ready for this.

2 Hua-Ling

Hua-Ling is 14. She met Zak at the fair and they've been seeing each other for three weeks. He is quite a bit older than her and really good looking – she's the envy of all her friends. Hua-Ling doesn't want to tell Zak how old she is. Zak says that she needs to trust him but she doesn't feel safe being alone with him.

3 Kojo

Kojo met Sandi at the club. They've been together for over a month. The two of them get on really well and Kojo's mates have accepted Sandi as a good friend too. When they've spent time alone there's been a lot of kissing but that's as far as things have gone. Recently Sandi has been suggesting they take things further – but Kojo doesn't feel ready to do this …

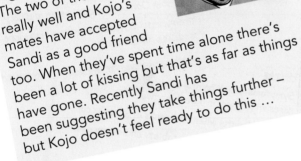

4 Rach

Rach is 13 and her parents are letting her have her 14th birthday party at home. They are going out for the evening and leaving Rach's older brothers, Nick and Dan, in charge. A great crowd is coming – and there will be as many boys as girls.

The evening goes really well. Nick and Dan are upstairs watching a DVD and downstairs Michael, who really fancies Rach, suggests they go up to her room – no one will notice. Rach fancies him too but this isn't what she wants.

It is natural to want to say yes to somebody to please them if they care about you they will understand you have your own feelings and wishes. Paying attention to your own feelings is not necessarily selfish.

English law states that people need to be 16 before they can choose to have a sexual relationship. Not that this means you *have* to have sex when you're 16. Despite what we might read about in newspapers and magazines, the majority of young people do wait until they are 16 or older to have sex.

'Early sex' can be defined as having sex before the age of 16 and before a person feels ready to.

Get Active 2

Imagine two young people like those in Source 3 are trying to decide whether to have or to delay having early sex. What reasons might they come up with in each case?

Source 3

Get Active 3

We all have the right to say 'no'. When responding this way to someone you care about, what responsibility comes with this right?

23 What are STIs?

> **In this lesson you will:**
> ★ **find out about sexually transmitted infections**
> ★ **learn some facts about condoms.**

'STI' stands for 'sexually transmitted infection'. These infections are mainly transmitted (that is passed from one person to another) during sex. There are at least 25 types of STI with a range of different symptoms.

Get Active 1

In pairs, decide whether you agree with, disagree with or are not sure about the statements in Source 1.

Source 1 STI quiz – Agree or disagree?

1	You can get STIs from toilet seats.
2	Chlamydia is the most common STI amongst teenagers in the UK.
3	You have to sleep around alot to get an STI.
4	You always know when you have an STI because it hurts when you pee.
5	All STIs can be cured.
6	You can only have one STI at a time.
7	A person with an STI is only infectious when they have symptoms.
8	STIs can cause infertility.
9	The only way to find out if you have an STI is to get tested.
10	Condoms provide protection against STIs.

Source 2 gives you some information about the six most important STIs to be aware of. These are the ones most likely to be transmitted amongst young people – and some have serious consequences.

Source 2 STI information

Chlamydia
Symptoms: Most people don't have any symptoms for a long time
Effects: Left untreated can cause infertility
Treatment: Antibiotics

Genital warts
Symptoms: Growths or warts in the genital area; they can take a year to appear after infection
Effects: Can be uncomfortable and ugly
Treatment: Ointments or freezing (done by medical professionals)

Herpes
Symptoms: Small painful blisters or sores which heal in a week or two
Effects: Painful when outbreaks of sores occur
Treatment: No cure but tablets and cream can reduce the severity

Pubic lice (crabs)
Symptoms: Pubic lice are not necessarily sexually transmitted but are usually passed on through close body contact; they can cause severe itching
Effects: No long-term health problems – but will only disappear if treated
Treatment: Special lotions which can be bought in pharmacies

Gonorrhoea
Symptoms: Most women and some men don't have any symptoms
Effects: Left untreated can cause problems including infertility
Treatment: Antibiotics

Syphilis
Symptoms: Sometimes none, sometimes a painless sore may appear within nine to ninety days, followed later by a rash and flu-like symptoms
Effects: If untreated may cause serious permanent health problems such as damage to the nervous system/dementia
Treatment: Antibiotics

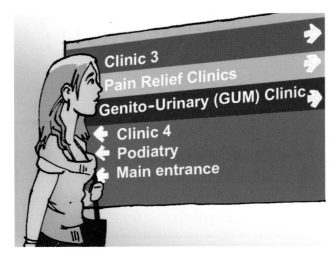

Knowing where your local GUM clinic is could be useful in the future. There is a wide range of free and confidential sexual health advice and contraception services for young people. They may be listed as: genito-urinary medicine (GUM) clinics; sexual health clinics; family planning clinics. Brook Advisory Centres – commonly known just as Brook – is a national voluntary provider of free and confidential sexual health advice and services specifically for young people under 25.

Condoms provide a simple and effective way of protecting against transmitting STIs – they can also be used as a contraceptive to prevent pregnancy.

However, condoms are only really effective if they are used properly. A condom is made of very thin latex (rubber) or polyurethane and fits over a man's erect penis. Condoms are lubricated to make them easier to use.

A condom acts as a barrier between the man and his partner. A condom covers the whole of the penis and stops sexual fluids being exchanged (semen or vaginal fluids). Condoms provide protection against sexually transmitted infections (STIs) as well as unwanted pregnancy. There will be instructions with the packet which usually have diagrams that show you how to put the condoms on.

Make sure the condom packet has a BSI or CE Kitemark which is a mark to show that it's been safety tested. You should also check the expiry date. Always use a new condom each time you have sexual contact.

Get Active 2

Condoms are 98 per cent effective when they are used correctly – this is a really important statement! What are the correct facts about how to use a condom?

Source 3 Condoms, the most widely used protective contraceptive

Three interesting things you might not know about condoms …

The ancient Egyptians used a type of condom in 1000BC

The first advertisement for condoms appeared in 1861 in the *New York Times*

A Durex condom can hold 40 litres of air, equivalent to 9 gallons of water

Get Active 3

Some advertisers find clever and funny slogans to remind us of their products such as in Source 4. What slogan can you think of to encourage people to use condoms?

'Soft, strong and very, very long'

'Melts in your mouth not in your hand'

'Have it your way'®

'Once you pop, you can't stop'

Source 4 Some advertising slogans

24 What is contraception?

In this lesson you will:
★ examine some facts and myths about contraception
★ investigate a variety of types of contraception
★ consider what advice you could give young people wanting to learn about contraception.

Starter activity

What do these two words mean?
● Conception
● Contraception

In the previous lesson you learnt about STIs and the most widely available type of contraception – the condom. When used properly, a condom is 98 per cent effective in preventing pregnancy.

'Properly' means:

● making sure that you squeeze the top of the closed end to get rid of any trapped air
● putting the condom on before starting to have sex
● using a new condom every time you have sex.

Source 1 Which of these methods protect against pregnancy?

1 The 'pill'	2 'If we do it standing up it'll be fine'	3 IUS
4 'IT'LL NEVER HAPPEN TO ME'	5 Emergency contraception pills	6 'It'll be OK the first time'
7 Contraceptive injection	8 Using cling film	9 Pulling out before coming
10 Having sex during a period	11 No sexual intercourse	12 Implant

Get Active 1

1 Working with a partner, look at Source 1 above and decide which of these methods protect against pregnancy.
2 Now see if you can match a picture (A–E) from Source 2 opposite to any of the genuine methods of contraception in Source 1.

Source 2 Contraceptives

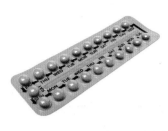
A

B

C

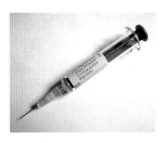
D

E

Get Active 2

What other methods of contraception have you heard of?

Get Active 3

Roz and Ike are both 17. They haven't had sex yet – they are planning to but have some questions they want answered first. They are thinking about going to their local sexual health clinic. Can you help answer their questions? You can check your advice against the information at www.brook.org.uk, www.teenagehealthfreak.org or using leaflets about services local to your area.

Source 3 Roz and Ike

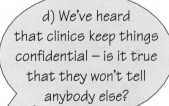

a) If we go to the clinic for advice before having sex won't they think we're wasting their time?

d) We've heard that clinics keep things confidential – is it true that they won't tell anybody else?

b) The clinic is a long way from where we live – can we go to see the doctor instead?

e) Will either of us have to have a physical examination before getting contraception?

c) Do we have to pay for the advice and the contraceptives?

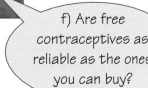

f) Are free contraceptives as reliable as the ones you can buy?

Get Active 4

Roz and Ike still have quite a lot to learn and so many things they are worried about. Would it be better for them to wait before having sex?

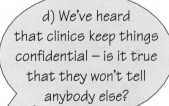

25 Is there equal respect?

In this lesson you will:
- ★ **think about whether boys and girls receive equal respect**
- ★ **consider a range of situations related to gender and stereotypes**
- ★ **apply this thinking to your own school and identify opportunities for change.**

Starter activity

Are boys and girls treated with equal fairness?
Give examples of situations where you think they are and situations where you think they aren't.

Get Active 1

Complete the statement 'If boys and girls treated each other fairly …' with as many endings as you can think of. For example:

'If boys and girls treated each other fairly … then boys would ask before they took over the whole playground for football.'

Think back to when you were younger and played with your own toys – what toys do boys remember playing with and what toys do girls remember playing with? Parents sometimes treat boys and girls differently. Parents may give toy trucks to boys and give dolls to girls. Parents may get upset if a boy picks up a doll and plays with it because they think a doll is a girl's toy. The same thing may happen when a girl plays with a toy truck or car.

The way the genders treat each other may stem from the fact that boys and girls are treated differently and don't naturally play together when they are young – and it takes time to learn to do this.

Get Active 2

Work in a small group to discuss and answer the following questions, thinking of examples to explain your answers:

1 Do you think boys get less affection at home as they are growing up? For example, are they hugged less just because they are boys?
2 Do parents expect less toughness and drive from a daughter than they would from a son?

Get Active 3

As they grow up boys are often encouraged to be 'macho' in their relationships, whilst girls in relationships are sometimes criticised for being either 'easy' or 'frigid'. Look at Source 1 below and work with others to decide where you stand on these statements. Is your answer to agree or disagree – or are you somewhere in the middle? Whatever your opinion, explain the reasons you have for holding this point of view.

Source 1
Do you think it's OK if …?

a) Men and women are paid differently for doing the same job.

b) Workmen on a building site whistle and shout at a woman walking by.

c) A woman is captain of a large aircraft.

d) A boy in school makes jokes about the size of a girl's breasts.

e) A man works as a nursery nurse.

f) A group of young men stare at and follow two young women in the street.

g) A group of girls make flirty comments about a guy's bum.

h) A father shows porn magazines to his son.

i) A father shows porn magazines to his daughter.

j) A judge at a rape trial says that women who say no to sex don't always mean no.

Get Active 4

'If you want to be respected by others the great thing is to respect yourself.'

Fedor Dostoevsky.

What could you do or say to show that you respect yourself?

26 How do we feel about 'difference'?

In this lesson you will:
★ reflect on 'difference' and what it means to individual people
★ consider how prejudice might be challenged
★ think about different types of relationships.

Source 1
Who are they?

A

B

C

D

E

F

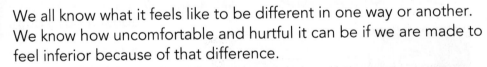

Starter activity

Look at Source 1. Can you name the people in the photographs? Can you spot a common link?

We all know what it feels like to be different in one way or another. We know how uncomfortable and hurtful it can be if we are made to feel inferior because of that difference.

In the worst cases a fear and hatred of people who are 'different' has led to events such as the Holocaust in the Second World War, the genocide in Rwanda (1994), 'ethnic cleansing' in the former Yugoslavia (1992) and, more recently, to the humanitarian crisis in Darfur in the Sudan (2003).

Recognising, understanding and accepting that there will always be similarities and differences between people may prevent ignorance, prejudice and fear from flourishing in the world.

Get Active 1

Read the three case studies in Source 2 opposite and in pairs discuss the following questions about one of them:

1 How would you feel if this happened to you?
2 Do you think the person in the case study has any options other than avoiding people? What are those options?
3 Is there any helpful advice you could give them?

Source 2 Feeling different

Peter

Whenever people ridiculed somebody or something they called it 'gay'; people's trainers, music – even pencils – got called 'gay'. We were all supposed to think that anything gay must be bad. For almost a year of my school life, I spent every break and lunchtime sitting in the back of the library reading because I knew I was safe there, that I was isolated, and no one would give me any hassle.

Peter is a young gay man.

Daniel

It was easy for me not to go to school. Mum and Dad worked and I often left the house after them and got back before them. They didn't know I was not going to school. I didn't do homework; the boys would take my bag off me when I got to school and throw the books about. When I didn't have my homework I couldn't tell the teacher it had been thrown away so I got into more trouble. It was better to stay at home.

Daniel has a learning disability.

Carmel

I liked my old school, but not my new school. In my old school I had lots of friends who were also black; in this school there are hardly any black people and none in my class. In lessons I feel OK, but I worry about break and dinner time when I get called all sorts of names. This is supposed to be a better school, but I don't like it and I want to go back to my old school.

Carmel is a young black woman.

Source 3
A famous poem urging people to speak out against prejudice. It is attributed to Martin Niemöller, a prominent anti-Nazi German pastor

> First they came for the communists, and I did not speak out
>   because I was not a communist;
> Then they came for the socialists, and I did not speak out
>   because I was not a socialist;
> Then they came for the trade unionists, and I did not speak out
>   because I was not a trade unionist;
> Then they came for the Jews, and I did not speak out
>   because I was not a Jew;
> Then they came for me
>   and there was no one left to speak out for me.

Get Active 2

Read the poem in Source 3. In speaking out against prejudice and hatred Martin Niemöller was trying to make an important point. Answer the following questions:

1 What do you think is the central message of the poem?
2 Who are the 'they' mentioned in the poem?
3 What does the poem have to do with our lives at school?
4 Why is it important to defend other people's rights?

Get Active 3

1 Rewrite the poem in Source 3 in the context of today – what groups of people do you feel should be included now?
2 Read the words of President Obama on the right. What golden rule could you make that would express your values towards other people?

As individuals we each value different things. President Barack Obama has spoken about our *common* values. He said, 'the call to love one another; to understand one another; to treat with dignity and respect those with whom we share a brief moment on this Earth' is the golden rule.

59

What do I need to know about drugs?

In this lesson you will:
★ **think about the use of drugs as medicines**
★ **find out about the Misuse of Drugs Act**
★ **identify situations where people may be breaking the law.**

Starter activity

Think back over what you have already learnt about drugs in your lessons at school. Work in pairs to come up with two important facts that you have learnt.

The likelihood is that you will have remembered a lot about the harm drugs can cause – but it's important to remember that some drugs are very helpful.

When drugs are licensed to be used as medicines in this country they have been through a series of trials to try to make sure they are as safe as possible. Some drugs are only available on prescription from a doctor and others can be bought 'over the counter' at a pharmacy.

Get Active 1

In groups of four:

• make a list of all the medicines you can think of
• choose two medicines from your list and for each one write down the benefits that using that drug could give and also some of the problems it might cause.

You should now be beginning to see that taking any drug (even medicines) may cause problems. For that reason society gives careful thought to the way it allows drugs to be used.

There is a law called the Misuse of Drugs Act which classifies drugs into three groups. These groups are called Class A, Class B and Class C. Each class carries different legal penalties for having the drugs or for selling them/giving them away.

Get Active 2

Here is a list of drugs which are covered by the Misuse of Drugs Act. Look at Source 1 and decide which class you think they belong in.

Amphetamines

Cannabis

Cocaine and crack cocaine

Ecstasy

Heroin

LSD

Magic mushrooms

Tranquillisers

Source 1 The Misuse of Drugs Act – maximum penalties

Class	Maximum penalty for possession (having them)	Maximum penalty for supplying (selling or giving them away)
A	Up to seven years in prison or an unlimited fine or both	Up to life in prison or an unlimited fine or both
B	Up to five years in prison or an unlimited fine or both	Up to 14 years in prison or an unlimited fine or both
C	Up to two years in prison or an unlimited fine or both	Up to 14 years in prison or an unlimited fine or both

The Misuse of Drugs Act does not cover all drugs. The Medicines Act covers the use and supply of medicines and there are other laws that control the use and supply of alcohol, tobacco and solvents.

Get Active 3

In each of the following situations, is anyone breaking the law? If so, identify who is breaking the law and how.

- Pat and Chris are 14. They are drinking cider on a street corner.
- Pradip is 14. He goes into Mrs Smith's shop and buys 20 cigarettes from her.
- 15-year-old Danni is with her friends in the shopping centre. She has some cannabis in her bag.
- Aasif and Dayo, both 15, are sitting in the park sniffing solvents.
- Lou is at a party and gives Jan an Ecstasy tablet which she accepts.

Get Active 4

Laws and facts about drugs are fairly complicated. There is a lot of misinformation and misunderstanding. Identify one new thing you have learnt today. How could it help you and your friends?

28 How do I manage situations involving drugs?

In this lesson you will:
★ **learn about the risks and effects of drugs**
★ **think about the way in which drug use may affect others as well as yourself**
★ **find ways to keep yourself and others safe.**

Here's a reminder of how we can define 'risk': *the chance of something bad happening.*

Risk is the chance that harm might be caused. When we think about risk we need to think about two things:

1 the *what* – the harm that might happen to us
2 the *might* – the likelihood that harm will happen to us.

One example is an aeroplane crashing. The chance of being harmed is high but the likelihood of this happening is low – very few planes crash compared to the large numbers that fly every day.

Starter activity

What events can you think of where drugs being present could lead to risky situations occurring? Think of one example for each of the following:

- **medicines**
- **alcohol**
- **solvents**
- **illegal drugs.**

Taking drugs is never risk free and different situations will present different levels of risk. Social situations may be risky because sometimes we leave it up to our friends to do the thinking for us.

Get Active 1

Look at Source 1 opposite. Working in pairs, come up with ideas about what is going on in the story. At first glance does it look as if any of the main characters are involved in risky behaviour? If so, what might they be?

Get Active 2

Think about the issues of risk and safety at the party in Source 1 opposite. In pairs, list the risks taken and then try to group them into different types of risk. For example, risks to health.

Get Active 3

Imagine you could sit down with one of the characters from the story and offer them a piece of good advice. What would it be?

Source 1 Chantelle, Mark and their friends – the party

Chantelle is invited with Mark, Surina and Rash to Jade's fifteenth birthday party.

We're relying on you two to keep an eye on things!

Jade's parents leave her older brother and sister in charge.

I only smoke about five a day so I can't be hooked on them.

Mark buys some cigarettes.

At the off licence …

Do you want some cider and breezers? Don't worry, they don't have much alcohol in …

I won't bother – it's against my religion and I can have a good time without it. Anyway it means I can keep an eye on the rest of you …

Rash tells them what he thinks.

Bet you a fiver I can down these in one go!

Mark, don't be stupid!

At the party Mark has a bet.

How about some punch?

What's in it?

Dunno – my sister made it.

There are lots of drinks to choose from.

You can't drink it on its own, have some of my vodka in it.

I'll have some juice.

How about some wine?

Chantelle has to decide.

'I wonder where Mark and Surina are …'

The party is underway.

Do you two want a smoke?

Some older guys chat them up.

How about some coffee?

Chantelle feels faint.

I should call my dad to come and get me.

I'll give you a lift, if you don't mind squeezing in my car – I'm going clubbing and it's on my way.

How will Chantelle get home?

Party scenario adapted for use from the Home Office's Blueprint programme Teacher Manual, Spring 2005.

29 Which drugs and what risks?

In this lesson you will:
★ consider different ways of looking at 'risk'
★ look at the various reasons people give for taking risks
★ reflect on the impact of risk-taking with drugs.

Name one rule or sanction about drugs in your school. (Remember 'drugs' refers to all drugs including medicines, volatile substances/ solvents, alcohol, tobacco and illegal drugs.)

Source 1

A Bungee jumping

B Parkour

C Texting to ask someone out on a date

D Speaking in front of your class

Get Active 1

Look at Source 1. For each of these situations answer the following questions:

1 Are there risks involved?
2 If there are risks, what are they?

Sometimes people take risks because they know or believe that the benefits they may possibly gain would outweigh any possible negative results. You could call this 'risking on purpose'. At times people do things on the spur of the moment without thinking through what might happen. They may be taking an 'unconsidered risk'.

Get Active 2

Now think about different drugs and why they might involve risks. Here are five statements designed to test your awareness on the topic of drugs and risks. Are the statements true or false?

1 Smoking only a few cigarettes a day is fine.
2 Alcohol slows down the brain.
3 Giving your own prescription medicines to someone else isn't a problem.
4 At least one young person a month dies from sniffing solvents.
5 You could be sent to prison for five years for being found with cannabis.

Despite all the information we have about drugs, people still take risks.

Different people have different reasons for taking risks with drugs. Here are some of the reasons people give:

- curiosity
- for a dare
- because they like the feeling
- to show off
- boredom
- to help someone
- because they are influenced by someone else.

Get Active 3

Look at the drugs listed in Source 2 below, then make a copy of the ladder, ranking the drugs on it with the one you think has the highest risk at the top and the one you think has the lowest risk at the bottom. Be ready to explain your decisions.

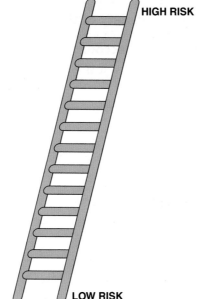

HIGH RISK

LOW RISK

Source 2

Alcohol
Amphetamines
Caffeine
Cannabis
Cocaine
Ecstasy
Heroin
LSD
Medicines – prescription
Medicines – shop-bought
Poppers
Solvents
Tobacco

Get Active 4

In this lesson you have been learning about drugs and risk. Identify something new that you have learnt about drugs and risk.

Who can I talk to about health problems?

In this lesson you will:
★ **identify some rights and ages of responsibility**
★ **think about the importance of 'confidentiality'**
★ **find out about your rights to health and treatment.**

The UK Government has agreed to uphold a set of international human rights for young people that mean:

● you should be treated with respect at all times
● you should be consulted whenever decisions are made about you
● you should never be treated unfairly because of your ethnic origin, sex, any disabilities, your religion or beliefs, your sexual orientation or your transgender status.

Source 1 Taken from a summary guide written by the Children's Rights Alliance: www.crae.org.uk/rights/uncrc.html

Starter activity

Look at Source 1 above – it outlines some key rights for young people. As you get older you gain other rights and become legally able to do a variety of things. At what age do you think you can:

1 **open a bank account in your own name?**
2 **get a part-time job – with some restrictions?**
3 **have a tattoo?**
4 **ride a moped of up to 50ccs?**

As a young person gains different rights they may realise that some of these rights involve sharing personal or sensitive information. We often want this information to be kept confidential.

Get Active 1

Read what the young people of different ages in Source 2 opposite have said about confidentiality. In pairs:

1 Discuss which of these definitions is the best.
2 Come up with your own definition of the word 'confidentiality'.

Age 11

Being able to talk to someone in private.

Not gossiping.

Age 12–13

When someone will not tell people about what you have said until you want them to.

Age 15–16

Very important … The information given by anyone should be kept in absolute trust.

When my information should only be shared with my permission.

Having the option to keep something private.

One of the situations where we want confidential care is when we see someone about personal health problems. Young people under 16 are entitled to have their confidential information treated in exactly the same way as adults. Your health care will more often than not be something you happily discuss with your parents. However, sometimes you may wish to discuss things in private.

Get Active 2

Look at Source 3 below. The photographs show young people using the health service. The questions in the speech bubbles are often asked by young people who are unsure of their rights. In groups, consider these worries. What would you say to reassure each questioner? You may find it helpful to refer back to Lesson 24 *What is contraception?* for some of the answers. The Brook website www.brook.org.uk will also help you answer these questions.

a) At what age can I see a doctor on my own?

Source 3 Seeing someone about your health

b) Can I choose my own doctor?

e) I think I have a problem but I'm not sure … What if the doctor thinks I'm wasting their time?

c) Can I be sure that I'll be treated in confidence by a nurse or doctor?

d) Can I get confidential advice about anything to do with sex if I'm under 16?

67

Get Active 3

In Source 4 below you will find some facts about a range of health services. Imagine your school council has asked for ideas of the best way to raise awareness of these services around school. How would you ensure as many pupils as possible could access the information?

In groups, come up with ideas on how you could raise awareness of the services by discussing the following questions:

1 What information would you need to provide?
2 How would you research this?
3 What method would you use to raise awareness (for example, posters, leaflets, web pages, etc.)?

Give feedback on your ideas to the class. Choose some of the best ideas and carry them out.

Source 4 Your agencies and choices

- **Pharmacies/chemists** offer services ranging from prescription dispensing to chlamydia screening and pregnancy testing. They can also advise on minor ailments. You can talk to your pharmacist in confidence and don't need to make an appointment.

- **Complementary therapy** or alternative medicines, such as acupuncture and homeopathy, are gradually becoming more widely available.

- If you don't know where to start you can ring the **NHS Direct** advice service. You will be put through to a trained nurse, who can give you information on all health-related issues. Children and young people are welcome to use their service and can give as many or as few personal details as they wish. Callers can also choose to remain anonymous. The service is also available online: www.nhsdirect.nhs.uk.

Although these agencies provide useful services, they aren't always substitutes for your GP. The NHS Direct service, for example, can't prescribe medical treatment or guarantee a totally accurate diagnosis over the phone. At best, these options should be used alongside a visit to your GP to discuss your choices.

Get Active 4

Complete this sentence: 'One useful piece of information I have gained from this lesson is …'

How far have I come?

In this lesson you will:
★ look at the end of Key Stage 3 statements for PSHE education
★ review what you have learnt against some of these statements
★ acknowledge your own skills, qualities and achievements.

Starter activity

Look at Source 1 – it should remind you of some of the topics you've covered in PSHE education this year. What has been the most memorable PSHE lesson for you this year? What made it memorable?

Source 1 An overview of PSHE education

Get Active 1

Copy and complete the table below to begin to show how far you think your learning has progressed in PSHE education. These are based on national ideas about what pupils your age need to be able to do. Give reasons and evidence to explain your responses.

I am able to …	Not yet developed	Need to practise more	Can do well
recognise when I experience strong emotions and manage them positively			
explain the characteristics of good health and know how to stay physically, emotionally and mentally healthy			
assess and manage risks associated with my personal lifestyle so that I can make safer choices			
negotiate with people in a range of relationships			
challenge prejudice and discrimination in an appropriate manner			
describe some of the qualities, attitudes and skills I will need for work in the future			
make informed decisions as a consumer of goods and services			
explain a range of basic economic and business terms			

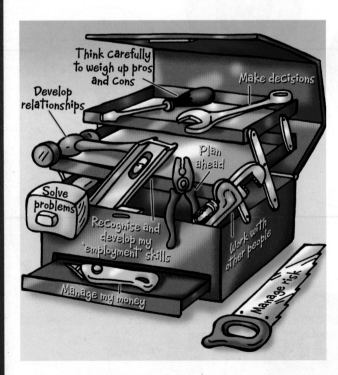

Source 2 My PSHE education toolbox

Get Active 2

Look at Source 2.

1 Imagine you have an empty toolbox. Which of the items/skills shown in Source 2 do you think you possess and could put in to *your* toolbox for Key Stage 4?
2 For each item you put in the box, describe a time or situation when you used that skill.

Get Active 3

Pick three ways to continue this sentence from the stems below and complete them for yourself.

In this year's PSHE education lessons …

I learnt that …
I really liked …
I didn't like …
I would have liked more of …
As a result of what I have learnt I will change …
I felt challenged when …